COOKIE STAGMAN'S

BEAUTIFUL BUFFETS

QUICK AND EASY PREPARATION

♦

SPICED WITH SPECIAL RECIPES
BY AMERICA'S TOP FASHION DESIGNERS

Happy Cooking & Enjoy!

Cookie Stagman

ARLENE MICHLIN BRONSTEIN
EDITOR

Cover Design:
Diane Kavelaras

Photography:
Curtis Kulp

Food Stylist:
Bonnie Rabert

Illustrations:
Geoff Allen
Ann O'Brien

Flowers:
Ronsley Florist, Chicago

Hair Stylist:
Bruce Ivan

Make-up Stylist:
Garry Vesper

First Edition Second Printing October, 1989

Printed in the United States of America
The Lakeside Press
R.R. Donnelley & Sons Company

Library of Congress Catalogue Card Number-89-091754
ISBN 0-9622983-0-1

DEDICATION

To my father, Fred Jawer, whose talent and creativity in the food business has always been an inspiration for me.

To my husband, Barry, who has encouraged me 100% of the way and has wanted to "taste it all"!

To my children, Jason and Lizzy, who always knew where to find me . . . in the kitchen!

And with great appreciation to Arlene Bronstein whose tenacity helped make this dream come true.

WITH SPECIAL THANKS . . . . . .

TO ALL THE TALENTED AMERICAN DESIGNERS WHO CONTRIBUTED
TO THIS BOOK:

Becky Bisoulis

Bill Blass

Eleanor P. Brenner

Oscar De La Renta

Louis Dell'Olio

James Galanos

Mark Heister

Carolina Herrera

Donna Karan

Barry and CeCe Kieselstein-Cord

Adrienne Landau

Ann Lawrence

Judith Leiber

Bob Mackie

Isaac Mizrahi

Nancy and David

Albert and Pearl Nipon

Maria Rodriguez

Carolyne Roehm

Sandra Roth

Arnold Scaasi

TO ALL THE WONDERFUL PEOPLE WHO TESTED MY RECIPES AND GAVE ME
GREAT SUGGESTIONS!

Penny Anixter, Ann Fiocchi, Suzy Fiocchi, Suzanne Friedman, Martin
Gapshis, Debbie Goodman, Shari Gray, Ilene Greenfield, Violet Gualandri,
Debbi Klein, Maureen Kotler, Zella Ludwig, Esther Michlin, Susie Ortner,
Robin Schultz and Marley Stein

A portion of the proceeds of this cookbook goes to The Special Olympics. By
supporting my efforts, you are also contributing to this worthy cause. Thanks!

CONTENTS

Not too long after the first lunch was served, people started asking me for my recipes. I have never turned down a single request. I was always complimented and was glad to share even my "secret" recipes. You can't imagine how much pleasure I get from hearing people tell me how much they enjoyed making the recipes for their family and friends. Soon people started telling me I should compile all the recipes in a book and I thought that sounded like a great idea. After many years of thinking about it, I finally decided that I was going to take the time to write down all my favorites. It has taken me nearly a year to get the entire book together, but I feel that it was time well spent.

As you can see by just reading through the table of contents, I have many more desserts than anything else. This is partly due to the fact that our showroom has no facility for heating foods, so everything I serve has to be cold, or at room temperature. It's also because I would rather eat sweets than anything else! Most of my recipes won't lower your cholesterol, but they will help to lift your spirits!

I have been collecting the recipes for about 20 years. Some of them are original, some of them have been handed down to me by relatives. A few of them have been given to me by good friends who share my love for cooking. I have been fortunate to have been surrounded by people who enjoy life, who love to "party" and yet feel the greatest warmth when in my kitchen. I am lucky to have a successful business, but I am very blessed to have a wonderful family and group of close friends that I love. To all of those special people who contributed to this collection, I say "THANKS!"

When I decided to make this a "market" cookbook, I thought it would be fun to include some of the recipes of our American Fashion Designer friends. They know what ingredients are important in a fabulous piece of clothing, and now you'll see that their talents extend to some wonderful edible ingredients as well. I am grateful for their participation in this project. They are truly the icing on my cake!

To you, the buyer, I say thanks for investing your time in the kitchen with my recipes. In this day and age, I know how important it is to make things that work. No one has any time to waste. Most of my recipes are very easy to do and require just a few steps. Most of the ingredients you'll probably have on hand or are easily found in your local grocery stores. I have also included some "tips" before each section of the book. I hope they will help you with all your cooking questions.

Now off to your kitchen . . . I hope you will enjoy these "quick and easy" recipes to create beautiful buffets for small family dinners up to large corporate events! Good health and good eating!

SOME HELPFUL HINTS

INSTANT EQUIVALENTS

Butter/Chocolate
- 2 tablespoons butter = 1 ounce
- 1 stick of butter = 1/2 cup
- 1 square of chocolate = 1 ounce

Crumbs
- 14 squares of graham crackers = 1 cup fine crumbs
- 19 chocolate wafers = 1 cup fine crumbs
- 1 slice of bread, dried = about 1/3 cup
- 4 ounces potato chips = 2 cups coarsely chopped

Fruits and Vegetables
- juice of 1 lemon = about 3 tablespoons
- grated peel of lemon = about 1 teaspoon
- juice of 1 orange = about 1/3 cup
- grated peel of orange = about 2 teaspoons
- 1 medium apple, chopped = about 1 cup
- 1 medium onion, chopped = about 1/2 cup
- 1 15 ounce box of raisins = 3 cups

Cream, cheese, eggs
- 1 cup whipping cream = 2 cups whipped
- 1 pound American cheese = 4 cups shredded
- 1/4 pound blue cheese = 1/2 cup crumbled
- 12-14 egg yolks = 1 cup
- 8-10 egg whites = 1 cup (see addendum)

Nuts
- 1 pound walnuts in shell = 1 1/2 - 1 3/4 cups shelled
- 1 pound almonds in shell = 3/4 to 1 cup shelled

Cream
- 1/2 pint sour cream = 1 cup
- 1/2 pound cottage cheese = 1 cup

SOME HANDY MEASUREMENTS

Dash = less than $1/8$ teaspoon

3 teaspoons = 1 tablespoon

4 tablespoons = $1/4$ cup

5 $1/3$ tablespoons = $1/3$ cup

8 tablespoons = $1/2$ cup

10 $2/3$ tablespoons = $2/3$ cup

12 tablespoons = $3/4$ cup

16 tablespoons = 1 cup

1 cup = 8 fluid ounces

1 cup = $1/2$ pint

2 cups = 1 pint

4 cups = 1 quart

4 quarts = 1 gallon

8 quarts = 1 peck

4 pecks = 1 bushel

1 liter = 1.06 quarts

NOTES

COOKIE'S COOKIES

COOKIE'S COOKIE TIPS

1. Check your oven temperature. You'd be surprised how "Off" it can be. Have it professionally calibrated.

2. Use only the freshest ingredients!

3. I use Grade A large eggs.

4. Margarine can easily be substituted for butter.

5. If the recipe calls for sweet butter and you only have salted, just reduce the amount of salt called for in the recipe or eliminate the salt completely.

6. Even when a recipe doesn't call for "greasing" the cookie sheets, I spray them anyway.

7. I bake my cookies on large, aluminum oven liners. If I bake smaller batches, I use regular shiny aluminum cookie sheets.

8. I use 2 teaspoons for drop cookies. I scoop with one and push the dough off onto the pan with the other.

9. Always leave about 3 inches between cookies. Most cookies spread a little.

10. For more uniform cookies, use a small ice cream scoop.

11. "Confectioners sugar" and "Powdered sugar" are the same thing. When using it as a garnish, I put it in a small can with a strainer top and then shake it to lightly dust the cookies or bars.

12. Do not overbake cookies! They become hard and dry. Better to underbake them and you'll have a moister, chewier cookie. Each oven is different (about a 25 degree variation) so watch the progress through the oven window. Opening the oven door can distort the cooking process.

13. Most of my cookies can be made ahead of time and frozen. I use heavy plastic containers or tin cans with air-tight lids. I line the bottom with wax paper and put it between the layers of cookies, too.

14. It is best to freeze each type of cookie separately. As cookies defrost, they contain different amount of moisture and this may change the texture of some cookies.

CANDY BAR COOKIES

Yield: 20-25 cookies   *Preheat oven to 350 degrees*

A child's delight, but oh how my buyers love them! These cookies freeze beautifully, and look as good as they taste! For my market, I triple this recipe.

½	cup sugar
½	cup brown sugar packed
½	cup butter or margarine
½	cup peanut butter
1	teaspoon vanilla extract
1	egg
1½	cups all purpose flour
½	teaspoon baking powder
½	teaspoon baking soda
10-15	mini Snicker or Milky Way Candy Bars (I split them in half)
20-25	wooden sucker sticks

In a large bowl, combine sugar, brown sugar, butter, peanut butter, vanilla extract and egg. Beat well. Add flour, baking powder and baking soda. Mix well. Cut candy bars in half and insert the stick to form a lollipop. Wrap enough dough around the candy bar to cover completely.

Place on a cookie sheet sprayed with non-stick cooking spray. Bake in a preheated 350 degree oven until light brown; about 12 minutes. Cool 10 minutes and remove from cookie sheet.

PEANUT BUTTER DOODLES

Yield: 40   *Preheat oven to 350 degrees*

This recipe was requested by the Chicago Sun-Times. It's a real favorite!

½	**cup butter**
½	**cup peanut butter**
½	**cup sugar**
½	**cup brown sugar**
1	**egg**
1	**teaspoon vanilla extract**
1½	**cups flour**
½	**teaspoon baking powder**
½	**teaspoon baking soda**
2	**9 ounce bags mini peanut butter cups**
	Mini muffin pans
	Mini muffin papers

Combine butter, peanut butter, sugar, brown sugar, egg and vanilla extract. Mix well.

Add the flour, baking powder and baking soda and blend well.

Spray mini muffin tins with non-stick cooking spray. Take a teaspoonful of dough and shape it in a ball. Press lightly into muffin tins. Bake for 10 - 12 minutes in a preheated 350 degree oven until light brown. Remove from oven and place 1 mini peanut butter cup into the middle of each muffin. Cool in the refrigerator and then remove from tins. Place in paper cups.

Freezes well.

P.S. You'll have about 10 mini peanut butter cups left over. I freeze them and enjoy them when I crave something sweet.

PIZZA COOKIE

Yield: 1 large cookie   *Preheat oven to 350 degrees*

This recipe looks like its name. Children can't believe it's a cookie and adults can't wait to eat it.

Crust:
  1   **cup butter**
  ½   **cup sugar**
  ½   **cup brown sugar**
  1   **egg**
  1   **teaspoon vanilla extract**
1¾   **cup flour**

Topping:
1½   **cup peanuts**
1½   **cup mini marshmallows**
16   **ounces chocolate chips**
25   **glazed baking cherries (I use S & W Red Glace Cherries - used for fruit cakes)**

  1   **14 inch pizza pan sprayed with non-stick cooking spray**

Mix butter, sugar and brown sugar until fluffy. Add egg and vanilla extract and beat well on low speed. Then slowly add flour and blend well.

Spread dough onto pizza pan and bake in a preheated 350 degree oven for 12 to 15 minutes until golden. Top cookie dough with nuts, marshmallows, chocolate chips and cherries to look like a pizza (cheese, meat & sausage). Return to oven until marshmallows melt. Cool slightly and cut with a pizza cutter into wedges or rectangles.

Alternative ways to use pizza dough, see the following recipe:
  Pizza Fruit Delight

Freezes well.

LEMON MERINGUE COOKIES

Yield: 20 cookies   *Preheat oven to 350 degrees*

This recipe can't be frozen, but it's a great treat and can be made the day before you need them.

- **2 egg whites**
- **⅔ cup sugar**
- **1 teaspoon lemon extract**
- **Cinnamon to taste (about ½ teaspoon)**
- **½ cup chopped pecans or walnuts**
- **6 ounces chocolate chips**

Beat egg whites on high speed until stiff. Gradually add sugar. Mix in all the remaining ingredients.

Line cookie sheets with aluminum foil and then spray with non-stick cooking spray (or use parchment paper). Drop dough by teaspoonfuls onto prepared sheets.

Place in a preheated 350 degree oven and immediately **TURN OFF HEAT**. Keep oven door closed and let cookies sit in oven at least 8 hours.**

** I make these cookies at night, before I go to bed. They are ready to eat the next morning!

OATMEAL CARAMEL COOKIES

Yield: 3 dozen cookies   *Preheat oven to 350 degrees*

Cookie mixture:
- 1   **cup all purpose flour**
- 1   **teaspoon baking soda**
- 1   **cup uncooked oatmeal**
- ¾ **cup brown sugar**
- ¾ **cup butter, melted**

Topping:
- 32 **caramels, melted**
- 5 **tablespoons evaporated milk**
- 1 **cup chocolate chips**
- ½ **cup chopped pecans**
- ¾ **cup caramel ice cream topping**
- 3 **tablespoons flour**

To make cookie mixture, combine flour, baking soda, oatmeal, brown sugar and melted butter. Press ½ of mixture into a 9 x 13 pan sprayed with non-stick cooking spray. Bake in a preheated 350 degree oven for 10 minutes.

While cookie mixture is baking, melt carmels in evaporated milk. Stir constantly to prevent burning. Remove cookie base and sprinkle with chocolate chips, nuts and melted caramels. Mix caramel ice cream topping with flour and pour over caramels. Top with rest of cookie mixture and press down slightly.

Return to oven and bake an additional 15-20 minutes. Cool completely before cutting into squares.

This recipe freezes well.

FROSTED CASHEW TOPPED COOKIES

Yield: 50 cookies   *Preheat oven to 350 degrees*

These are one of my husband Barry's favorites, so I have to freeze them as soon as they are baked or I won't have them for the market.

1	**cup firmly packed brown sugar**
½	**cup butter (do not use margarine or other substitute)**
½	**teaspoon vanilla extract**
1	**egg**
2	**cups all purpose flour**
¾	**teaspoon baking powder**
¾	**teaspoon baking soda**
⅓	**cup sour cream**
¾	**cup chopped cashew nuts**

Frosting

½	**cup butter**
2	**cups confectioners sugar**
3	**tablespoons half and half**
½	**teaspoon vanilla**
2	**6 ounce bags whole cashew nuts for garnish**

In large bowl, beat butter and sugar until light and fluffy. Add vanilla extract and egg; beat well. Add flour, baking powder, baking soda and sour cream. Mix well. Add chopped nuts. Blend.

Spray cookie sheets with non-stick cooking spray. Drop by spoonfuls onto prepared baking sheet and bake in a preheated 350 degree oven for 8-10 minutes. Remove cookies and cool.

Frosting: In a medium sauce pan, lightly brown butter and remove from heat. Stir in confectioners sugar, half and half and vanilla extract. Beat until smooth. Frost cooled cookies and top each with a cashew.

This recipe freezes well.

GRANDMA ESTHER'S RUGALAH

Yield: 40-45 pieces   *Preheat oven to 350 degrees*

Dough:
    4   cups all purpose flour, sifted
    1   cup butter or margarine (2 sticks)
    1   cup sour cream (8 ounces)
    2   egg yolks (reserve whites)
        vegetable oil for greasing hands

Cut butter into flour with pastry cutter or 2 knives. Add rest of ingredients, mix well with a wooden spoon as far as you can. Lightly oil your hands and continue to mix dough until you can form a ball. (After cutting in butter, the last steps can be done in a heavy duty mixer.)

Divide into 4 balls. Wrap each in wax paper. Refrigerate about 1 hour.

Cover reserved egg whites and refrigerate.

Remove dough from refrigerator and let soften. Roll dough out on lightly floured board to form a circle if you wish to make crescents, or into a large rectangle if you want the rugalah in the form of strudel. Dough should be thin.

Filling:
    1   stick melted butter or margarine
    2   teaspoons cinnamon
    1   cup sugar
  1½   cups chopped walnuts
   ½   cup white raisins

Brush dough with melted butter or margarine.

Mix cinnamon, sugar, nuts and raisins together. Sprinkle over melted margarine.

Cut dough into 12-16 wedges. Roll up in crescents with point tucked under or roll up jelly-roll fashion like strudel, fold ends under and cut in 1 inch slices. Place on ungreased cookie sheets. Brush with lightly beaten egg whites.

Topping:
  ¾ **cup sugar**
  1 **teaspoon cinnamon, scant**

Mix sugar and cinnamon and sprinkle on rolled up dough.

Bake 20 to 25 minutes or until brown in a preheated 350 degree oven.

ZELLA'S COOKIES

Yield: 60 to 70 cookies   *Preheat oven to 375 degrees*

These cookies were given to me by the wonderful lady who typed up all my recipes for the book. Thanks, Zella!

2½	**cups flour**
½	**teaspoon salt**
1	**teaspoon baking soda**
1	**teaspoon baking powder**
1	**cup butter or margarine**
1	**cup brown sugar, packed**
1	**cup white sugar**
2	**eggs**
2	**teaspoons vanilla extract**
2	**cups oatmeal, pulverized**
14	**ounces chocolate chips**
1½	**cups chopped nuts, walnuts or pecans**

Sift flour, salt, baking soda and baking powder.

Cream butter and sugars. Add eggs and vanilla extract.

Add sifted ingredients, then oatmeal, chocolate chips and nuts.

Refrigerate for 1 hour. Roll into walnut sized balls and place on ungreased cookie sheet, 2 inches apart.

Bake in preheated 375 degree oven for 8 minutes.

BRYN MAWR'S SECRET COOKIES

This cookie used to be made with the kitchen door closed, so no one could see how they were made at Bryn Mawr Country Club. But, when the baker was replaced, the recipe got out and I was lucky enough to get it from my friend Terri D!

3	**cups firmly packed confectioners sugar**
7	**tablespoons cocoa**
2	**tablespoons flour**
3	**egg whites**
2	**cups chopped pecans**
	Parchment paper

In a medium bowl, combine sugar, cocoa and flour. Add egg whites and beat on a high speed for 1 minute. Turn speed down to low and stir in nuts.

Line cookie sheets with parchment paper. Drop scant teaspoon sized cookies onto pans. Bake in a preheated 350 degree oven for 15 minutes. (Bake only 10 minutes for a chewier cookie.) Cool on parchment before removing.

This recipe should **NOT BE FROZEN**. The cookies should be stored in an airtight container and are best eaten right out of the oven!

FLORENTINE COOKIES

Yield: 30 small cookies   *Preheat oven to 325 degrees*

- **2 cups Quick Quaker Oats**
- **1 tablespoon flour**
- **2 cups sugar**
- **½ teaspoon salt (optional)**
- **2 sticks melted butter**
- **2 eggs, beaten**
- **1 teaspoon vanilla extract**

Mix dry ingredients together. Pour hot butter over dry ingredients and stir until sugar is dissolved. Add eggs and vanilla extract. Stir well.

Line cookie sheet with aluminum foil. Drop by ½ teaspoons of dough 3 inches apart. Bake in a preheated 325 degree oven for 12 minutes. Cool for 10 minutes before removing from the cookie sheet.

KRUNCHY KRISPIES

Yield: 30 squares

- **12 ounces butterscotch chips**
- **1 cup creamy peanut butter (or cashew butter is terrific)**
- **6 cups Rice Krispies cereal**

In a double boiler, melt butterscotch chips and peanut butter. When melted, mix in Rice Krispies cereal. Pour onto a wax paper lined 9 x 13 x 2 pan sprayed with non-stick cooking spray (or line it with foil paper). Use wax paper to help pat mixture down into pan until it reaches the corners and is flat. Chill for 1 hour and then cut into squares.

TURTLE COOKIES

Yield: 30 cookies   *Preheat oven to 325 degrees*

This recipe takes a little longer than most, but like the turtle, it's a real winner in the end!

Cookie dough:
1¼	sticks of butter or margarine
⅔	cup brown sugar, firmly packed
1	large egg
1	teaspoon vanilla extract
1¾	cup all purpose flour
½	teaspoon baking powder
½	teaspoon baking soda

Topping:
2	10 ounce packages of pecan halves
20	marshmallows cut in half
6	ounces semi sweet chocolate chips
1	12 ounce jar caramel sauce

———————————

Cream butter and sugar until light and fluffy. Beat in egg and vanilla extract. Add flour, baking powder and baking soda. Mix until well blended.

For each "turtle", place 4 pecans on sprayed cookie sheets in an "X" shape. Take about a 1 inch ball of dough and press onto pecans. Bake about 10 minutes in a preheated 325 degree oven. Take out of oven when dough turns a light brown. Add a small amount of caramel sauce. On top of sauce press down a marshmallow half. Place back in oven until marshmallow melts. Take out of oven immediately and press marshmallow down with your hand once again. (Be careful not to burn yourself.)

Melt the 6 ounces of chocolate chips. Dip turtle cookies into melted chocolate chips so that just the marshmallow is covered. Place cookies on wax paper until the chocolate hardens.

** The basic cookie dough is delicious just for sugar cookies.

PEANUT MARSHMALLOW CHEWS

Yield: 36 pieces   *Preheat oven to 350 degrees*

Crust:
- 1½ cups all purpose flour
- ⅔ cup firmly packed brown sugar
- ½ teaspoon baking powder
- ¼ teaspoon salt
- ¼ teaspoon baking soda
- ½ cup butter or margarine
- 1 teaspoon vanilla extract
- 2 egg yolks
- 3 cups miniature marshmallows

Topping:
- ⅔ cup corn syrup
- ⅓ cup butter or margarine
- 2 teaspoons vanilla extract
- 12 ounces (2 cups) peanut butter chips
- 2 cups Rice Krispies cereal
- 2 cups salted peanuts (1 - 12 ounce can)

Spray a 9 x 13 pan with non-stick cooking spray.

In a large bowl, combine all ingredients for the crust, except marshmallows. Beat on a low speed until crumbly. Firmly press crust into prepared pan.

Bake in a preheated 350 degree oven for 12 to 15 minutes or until light golden brown. Immediately sprinkle with marshmallows and return to the oven for 1 to 2 minutes until marshmallows puff. Be sure to watch closely or the marshmallows will burn. Remove from oven and cool while preparing topping.

In a large sauce pan, heat corn syrup, ⅓ cup butter or margarine, 2 teaspoons vanilla extract and peanut butter chips. Stir constantly until smooth. Remove from heat. Stir in cereal and nuts. Immediately spoon mixture onto marshmallows to cover.

Refrigerate until firm, then cut into bars.

This recipe can be frozen.

CINNAMON CARAMEL COOKIES

Yield: 48 cookies   *Preheat oven to 350 degrees*

These cookies are quick, easy and delicious!

24	**cinnamon graham cracker squares**
½	**pound of butter or margarine**
1	**cup brown sugar, firmly packed**
1½	**cups chopped walnuts or pecans**

Spray non-stick cooking spray on a large cookie sheet that has sides. Place all 24 cinnamon graham crackers on the pan. In a heavy sauce pan, over low heat, melt butter (or margarine) and brown sugar. Bring to a boil and stir constantly for approximately 4-5 minutes or until it caramelizes. Pour the mixture evenly over cinnamon graham crackers. Sprinkle the top with chopped nuts.

Bake in a preheated 350 degree oven for 10 minutes. Cool for 10 minutes. Cut each square in half. There should be 2 rectangular cookies for each square. (If I want very small cookies, I sometimes cut each cookie into 4 pieces.)

SHORT BREAD COOKIES

Yield: 45 cookies   *Preheat oven to 350 degrees*

2	cups sifted flour
1/3	cup corn starch
1/2	cup sugar
1/2	pound butter
1/2	teaspoon vanilla extract
3 1/2	ounces ground walnuts

Mix all of the ingredients together. Flour both your rolling pin and the surface where you'll be rolling out the dough to prevent it from sticking. I use a heart shaped cookie cutter, but any simple shape will do.

Spray cookie sheets with non-stick cooking spray. Bake in a preheated 350 degree oven for 15-20 minutes, until light brown.

P.S. When I'm very lazy I put all the batter on a jelly roll pan and pat it down. I bake it 25 minutes until light brown and then cut it into squares.

DEEP CHOCOLATE FUDGE DROPS

Yield: 30 cookies

1	cup semi-sweet chocolate chips
1	cup butterscotch pieces or chips
1 1/4	cups Quaker Natural cereal
1	cup peanuts, chopped

Melt chocolate and butterscotch chips in the top of a double boiler. Remove from heat and stir in cereal and nuts.

Drop by teaspoons on wax paper lined pans. Chill in refrigerator until firm.

JAIME AND ABBY'S PEANUT BUTTER COOKIES

Yield: 24 cookies   *Preheat oven to 350 degrees*

These cookies are so easy that the kids love to make them by themselves.

³⁄₄	**cup creamy peanut butter**
1	**stick margarine**
1¼	**cups flour**
½	**cup sugar**
½	**cup brown sugar, firmly packed**
1	**egg**
1	**teaspoon baking soda**
¼	**teaspoon baking powder**
	pinch of salt

Cream peanut butter and margarine. Slowly add rest of ingredients just until dough is firm.

Spray cookie sheet with non-stick cooking spray. Drop cookies by spoonfuls. Lightly press each cookie with fork to create grooves. Bake in a preheated 350 degree oven for 10-12 minutes.

JELLY BUTTONS

I always double this recipe because it's one of the market favorites. People can't believe it's made with hard boiled eggs!

½	**pound butter**
2	**hard boiled egg yolks**
¾	**cup sugar**
2¼	**cups flour**
	Raspberry and apricot preserves (or any other flavor preserve)

Cream together all ingredients except preserves. Add flour on low speed. Using your hand, roll dough into a cylinder-like form. Divide dough into 4 equal parts. Cut into ½ inch pieces and indent each to look like a thumb was stuck in the middle. Fill the indentation with the preserves.

Place on a cookie sheet sprayed with non-stick cooking spray and bake 12 minutes in a preheated 350 degrees or until light brown.

INCREDIBLE CHOCOLATE CHIP COOKIES

Yield: 48 cookies   *Preheat oven to 350 degrees*

These cookies are huge! They are delicious out of the oven or right out of the freezer.

½	cup butter, softened
1½	cups butter flavored Crisco
1½	cups brown sugar
1	cup sugar
4	eggs
1	teaspoon vanilla extract
3½	cups flour
2	teaspoons baking powder
2	teaspoons baking soda
1½	cups regular oatmeal
16	ounces chocolate chips
	(Chocolate chunks may replace chips)
	nuts (optional)

Beat butter, Crisco, brown sugar, and sugar until fluffy, add eggs and vanilla extract and continue beating until creamy. Combine all dry ingredients and add to creamed mixture. Mix in chips and nuts.

Drop by tablespoon onto cookie sheets sprayed with non-stick cooking spray. Leave room because they expand. Bake 10-12 minutes in a preheated 350 degree oven. Let cool a few minutes before removing from cookie sheet.

These cookies freeze well.

MELTING MOUTHFULS

Yield: 50 cookies   *Preheat oven to 325 degrees*

- ¾ **cup butter**
- 1 **teaspoon vanilla extract**
- 1 **cup flour**
- ½ **cup sugar**
- ¼ **cup corn starch**
- **Variety of colored sugar sprinkles**

Cream together butter and vanilla extract. Add flour, sugar and corn starch. Break off pieces of dough and roll into little balls. Take balls and roll them into colored sugar.

Place on a cookie sheet sprayed with non-stick cooking spray. Bake in a preheated 325 degree oven for 10 minutes. Cool on a wire rack.

WORLD'S BEST COCONUT MACAROONS

Yield: 20 macaroons   *Preheat oven to 325 degrees*

- 1 **tablespoon + 2 teaspoons butter, melted**
- 2⅔ **cups coconut**
- ¾ **cup sweet condensed milk**
- 1 **egg, beaten slightly**
- ¼ **teaspoon vanilla extract**

Optional: 1 square melted chocolate for chocolate macaroons.

Mix all ingredients together in a large bowl with a large spoon. Drop by spoonfuls onto a cookie sheet sprayed with non-stick cooking spray.

Bake in a preheated 325 degree oven for approximately 20 minutes or until light brown. Remove from oven immediately and cool.

ANNE'S OATMEAL CHOCOLATE CHIP COOKIES

Yield: 48 cookies   *Preheat oven to 375 degrees*

Cream:
- 2 cups corn oil margarine (room temperature)
- 2 cups sugar
- 2 cups brown sugar

Add:
- 4 eggs (room temperature)
- 2 teaspoons vanilla extract

Mix in:
- 4 cups flour
- 4¼ cups oatmeal - pulverized in processor
- 1 teaspoon salt
- 2 teaspoons baking powder
- 2 teaspoons baking soda

Add to above mixture:
- 24 ounces chocolate chips
- 1 8 ounce plain Hershey Bar - finely grated in processor
- 6 ounces chopped nuts, any kind (optional)

Roll dough to size of golf balls. Place on ungreased cookie sheets, 2 inches apart. Balls may be flattened a little.

Bake in a preheated 375 degree oven for 10 to 12 minutes.

DON'T OVERBAKE! DO NOT LET COOKIES TURN BROWN IN OVEN!

Let cool on cookie sheet for 3-5 minutes and then cool on rack.

BLACK BOTTOM MUFFINS

Yield: 4 dozen   *Preheat oven to 350 degrees*

My friend Barb gave me this recipe for market. It's always a hit!

Bottom:
1½   **cups flour**
1   **cup sugar**
¼   **cup cocoa**
1   **teaspoon baking soda**
½   **teaspoon salt**
1   **cup water**
⅓   **cup oil**
1   **tablespoon vinegar**
1   **teaspoon vanilla extract**

Filling:
1   **8 ounce cream cheese**
1   **egg**
⅓   **cup sugar**
       Pinch of salt (optional)
1   **cup chocolate chips**

To prepare the "bottom", pour sifted flour into a mixing bowl. Add sugar, cocoa, baking soda and salt. Mix well. Add water, oil, vinegar and vanilla extract and beat until well blended. Set aside.

To prepare the "filling", beat cream cheese well and then add egg, sugar, and salt. Add chocolate chips and stir until blended.

Spray mini-muffin tins with non-stick cooking spray or line each with a paper cup. Fill ⅔ of cup with "bottom" mixture and top with "filling" mixture (approximately ½ teaspoon).

Bake in a preheated 350 degree oven for 20 minutes. Test for doneness with a toothpick.

These muffins freeze well.

WHITE CHOCOLATE CHUNK COOKIES

Yield: About 50 cookies   *Preheat oven to 350 degrees*

Freezes well.

2¼	**cups all purpose flour**
⅔	**cup cocoa (I use Hershey's, but any brand will do)**
1	**teaspoon baking soda**
½	**teaspoon salt (optional)**
1⅓	**cups butter**
1	**cup sugar**
⅔	**cup firmly packed brown sugar**
2	**teaspoons vanilla extract**
2	**eggs**
1½	**cups white chocolate baking pieces**

Use non-stick cooking spray on all baking sheets.

In a small bowl, combine flour, cocoa, baking soda and salt; set aside. In a large bowl combine butter, sugars and vanilla extract and beat well. Add eggs, one at a time, beating well after each addition. Gradually add flour mixture. Slowly beat in white chocolate pieces. Drop by rounded teaspoons onto prepared cookie sheets.

Bake in a preheated 350 degree oven for 8 to 10 minutes. Cool 4 minutes and remove from cookie sheet.

MELT IN YOUR MOUTH HAMENTASCHEN

Yield: 20   *Preheat oven to 350 degrees*

Dough:
- 1   stick butter
- 1   cup sugar
- 1   egg, beaten
- 2   tablespoons orange juice
- 1   teaspoon vanilla extract
- 2½ cups pre-sifted flour
- 2   teaspoons baking powder

Filling:
Preserves: any flavor your family would like. I use apricot, raspberry and blueberry. You can substitute chocolate chips, or prune, poppy seed or almond filling.

Cream butter and sugar. Add beaten egg. Blend in orange juice and vanilla extract. Add flour and baking powder and mix well. Put dough in refrigerator for at least 3 hours.

Flour a flat surface and roll dough out. Use a circle cookie cutter to cut out the shapes. Add filling to each circle and fold up into a 3 cornered cookie. Pinch corners to hold shape. This will make mini cookies. Use a glass or jar top to increase the size.

Place on a cookie sheet sprayed with non-stick cooking spray. Bake in a preheated 350 degree oven for 20 minutes or until light brown.

Freezes well.

CRUNCHY POPPY SEED COOKIES

Yield: 5 dozen cookies   *Preheat oven to 350 degrees*

- ½ **pound butter**
- 1½ **cups confectioners sugar**
- 2 **eggs**
- 3 **cups flour**
- 2 **teaspoons vanilla extract**
- 4 **tablespoons poppy seeds**

Cream butter and sugar. Add eggs and blend well. Mix in the flour. Add vanilla extract and poppy seeds.

Roll the dough into small balls and place on a sprayed cookie sheet. Flatten each ball with a fork.

Bake in a preheated 350 degree oven for 15 minutes or until light brown.

Freezes well.

ALMOND COOKIES

Yield: 30 cookies   *Preheat oven to 325 degrees*

- 1 **8 ounce can of almond paste**
- 1¼ **cups sugar**
- 2 **egg whites**

In a medium sized mixing bowl cut almond paste into small pieces. Beat in sugar and egg whites.

Grease cookie sheets and drop cookies in ½ teaspoon amounts approximately a ½ inch apart. Bake in a preheated 325 degree oven for 25-30 minutes until light brown and dry. Cool well before storing or freezing.

GRANDMA JEAN'S BUTTER CRESCENTS

Yield: 40 cookies   *Preheat oven to 350 degrees*

This is my mother's recipe - my daughter Lizzy's favorite. In fact, it is everyone's favorite. It's impossible to eat just one. I always double this recipe.

 1 **cup butter**
 ½ **cup brown sugar**
 2 **cups flour, sifted**
 ¼ **teaspoon salt (optional)**
 1 **tablespoon water**
 1 **teaspoon vanilla extract**
 2 **cups finely chopped pecans**
    Confectioners sugar (for sprinkling on top of cooled cookies)

Cream butter. Add sugar, gradually. Blend well.   Add sifted flour, salt, water and vanilla extract. Add chopped nuts and blend well. Break off small pieces of dough and form into small half moons.

Place on sprayed cookie sheets. Bake in a preheated 350 degree oven for 15 to 18 minutes. Cool and sprinkle with confectioners sugar.

HERSHEY SQUARE SPRITZ COOKIES

Yield: 32 cookies   *Preheat oven to 350 degrees*

1	**cup butter, softened**
3/4	**cup sugar**
3	**large egg yolks**
1	**teaspoon vanilla extract**
2 1/4	**cups all purpose flour**
5	**Hershey Bars**

Beat butter well. Gradually add sugar and beat about 5 minutes until light and fluffy. Add egg yolks and vanilla extract and beat well. Gradually add flour. The dough should be stiff.

Fill an electric cookie gun with about half the dough. Using the ribbon disc, shoot out dough in strips on a sprayed cookie sheet. Break off little squares of Hershey chocolate bars and line them up vertically on the strips of dough. Fill cookie gun with remaining half of dough and shoot out strips to cover the Hershey Bar pieces.

Bake in a preheated 350 degree oven for 8 to 10 minutes. Cool the strips on the cookie sheet and then cut into squares.

KAREN'S PEANUT BUTTER BALLS

Yield: 75-90 balls

½	pound crushed graham crackers
½	pound butter, softened
1	box confectioners sugar
12	ounce jar crunchy peanut butter
1	teaspoon vanilla extract
½	bar paraffin wax
12	ounces chocolate chips

Mix together graham cracker crumbs, butter, confectioners sugar, peanut butter and vanilla extract. Blend well. Then shape dough into small balls.

In a double boiler, melt wax and chocolate chips. Dip each ball into melted mixture and cover using a wooden spoon. Place on wax paper lined cookie sheets until chocolate hardens. Store between sheets of wax paper in a plastic or Tupperware container.

Freezes well.

HEAVENLY HASH

1½	12 ounce packages of milk chocolate chips
½	12 ounce package of semi sweet chips
1	12 ounce jar crunchy peanut butter
6	ounces mini marshmallows

In an uncovered double boiler, melt the chocolate chips and peanut butter. Stir until smooth and melted. Add the mini marshmallows and stir to coat. Pour into a 9 x 13 pan sprayed with non-stick cooking spray.

Chill and cut into squares.

I put them into mini paper cups before freezing or serving.

CHOCOLATE BUTTONS

¼   cup butter or margarine
4   ounces (4 squares) unsweetened chocolate melted or 4 pre-melted
      packets unsweetened or baking chocolate
2   cups all purpose flour
2   cups sugar
2   teaspoons baking powder
3   eggs
½   cup chopped walnuts
      Confectioners sugar

In a sauce pan, melt margarine and chocolate over low heat. Stir constantly. Remove from heat and cool slightly. In a blender mix flour, sugar, baking powder and eggs. Add butter and chocolate mixture on low speed. Add chopped walnuts and stir just until blended.

Chill dough in the refrigerator for 30 minutes. Break off small pieces of dough and shape into 1 inch balls. Roll in confectioners sugar and coat heavily. Place balls 2 inches apart on a sprayed or greased cookie sheet. Bake 15 to 18 minutes in a preheated 300 degree oven or until edges are light brown. Immediately remove from cookie sheet.

Freezes well.

MERINGUE RUGALAH

Yield: 60 pieces   *Preheat oven to 400 degrees*

Dough
- 4 **cups flour**
- 1/2 **pound butter or margarine**
- 1/4 **ounce dry yeast (1 package)**
- 3 **egg yolks, slightly beaten (reserve whites)**
- 1/2 **cup sour cream**
- 1 **teaspoon vanilla extract**
  Confectioners sugar for dusting

Filling
- 3 **egg whites**
- 1 **cup sugar**
- 1 **teaspoon vanilla extract**
- 1 **cup chopped walnuts**

Cut butter into flour with pastry cutter. Sprinkle yeast into butter/flour mixture. Mix rest of ingredients together to form dough. Dough may be crumbly. Divide into 4 balls. Wrap in wax paper and refrigerate over-night or place in freezer for 1 hour. Cover reserved egg whites and refrigerate.

Dust board with confectioners sugar. Roll out each piece and cut in two (8 pieces total). Roll into thin, large rounds.

Prepare filling by beating egg whites until small peaks begin to form. Slowly add sugar and vanilla extract. Continue beating until stiff, but not dry. Stir in walnuts. Spread filling over dough.

Cut into small or large wedges. Roll up from large side to small point. Tuck point under. Place on greased cookie sheets.

Bake 15 to 20 minutes in a preheated 400 degree oven.

Cool on racks.

SNICKER DOODLE

Yield: 48 cookies   *Preheat oven to 350 degrees*

These little crunch cookies are my husband's favorite. They are hard to stop eating when you start. Great with coffee or a cup of tea.

1½   **cups sugar**
 ½   **cup butter or margarine**
 2   **eggs**
 1   **teaspoon vanilla extract**
2¾   **cups all purpose flour**
 1   **teaspoon cream of tartar**
 ½   **teaspoon baking soda**

Topping:
 2   **tablespoons sugar**
 2   **teaspoons cinnamon**
     Mix above together (add more if needed for topping)

In a large bowl cream sugar and butter. Add eggs and vanilla extract and mix well. Add flour, cream of tartar and baking soda. Mix until dough forms.

Break off small pieces of dough and shape into 1 inch balls. Roll in the sugar and cinnamon mixture. Place about 2 inches apart on greased or sprayed cookie sheet. In a preheated 350 degree oven, bake for 8 to 10 minutes or until light brown. Immediately remove from cookie sheet.

Freezes well.

BROWNIE DROP COOKIES

Yield: 24 cookies   *Preheat oven to 350 degrees*

2	bars German sweet chocolate
1	tablespoon butter
2	eggs
3/4	cup sugar
1/4	cup unsifted flour
1/4	teaspoon baking powder
1/4	teaspoon cinnamon
1/2	teaspoon vanilla extract
3/4	cup chopped nuts

Melt chocolate and butter in a double boiler. Stir and set aside to cool.

In a separate bowl, beat eggs until foamy. Add sugar, 2 tablespoons at a time. Beat until thickened, approximately 5 minutes. Blend in cooled chocolate. Add flour, baking powder and cinnamon. Stir in vanilla extract and nuts.

Drop onto a greased cookie sheet and bake in a preheated 350 degree oven for 8-10 minutes.

These cookies freeze well.

CHOCOLATE PECAN CLUSTERS

Yield: 24 cookies   *Preheat oven to 350 degrees*

2	squares unsweetened chocolate, melted
½	cup butter
1	cup sugar
2	eggs
2½	teaspoons vanilla extract
1	cup flour
½	teaspoon baking powder
1	package chopped pecans
1	package caramels
1-2	tablespoons milk

Melt chocolate. Set aside to cool.

Cream butter and sugar. Add eggs and blend well. Add vanilla extract and cooled chocolate. Slowly mix in the flour, baking powder and pecans. Mix well.

Drop dough by teaspoonful onto a greased cookie sheet. Bake in a preheated 350 degree oven for 10 minutes. Cookies should be soft.

While cookies are cooling, melt the caramels in a double boiler. When they start to melt, add milk and stir often to prevent burning. (Adjust the amount of milk to make caramels spreading consistency.) Frost cooled cookies with caramel mixture.

Freezes well.

CHOCOLATE CHEWS

Yield: 25 cookies   *Preheat oven to 350 degrees*

- 1   **12 ounce package of chocolate chips**
- ½   **stick butter**
- 1   **can Eagle Brand Sweet Condensed Milk**
- 1   **cup flour**
- 1   **cup chopped walnuts or pecans**
- 1   **teaspoon vanilla extract**

Melt chips, butter and milk in top of double boiler. Remove from heat. In the same pot add the flour, nuts and vanilla extract. Mix well.

Drop by teaspoons on a cookie sheet sprayed with non-stick cooking spray. Bake in a preheated 350 degree oven for 7 minutes. Cool cookies on a wire rack.

MEXICAN WEDDING COOKIES

Yield: 24 cookies   *Preheat oven to 350 degrees*

- ½   **pound butter**
- 4   **tablespoons confectioners sugar**
- 2   **cups sifted flour**
- 2   **cups pecans, chopped fine**
- 2   **teaspoons vanilla extract**

Mix all ingredients together. Roll dough into small balls and place on a sprayed cookie sheet.

Bake in a preheated 350 degree oven until light brown, 10-12 minutes. Cool and roll in confectioners sugar.

ELEGANT LACE COOKIES

Yield: 24 cookies   *Preheat oven to 350 degrees*

¼	**pound melted butter**
½	**cup + 2 tablespoons sugar**
1	**cup + 2 tablespoons quick oatmeal**
1	**tablespoon flour**
1	**teaspoon baking powder**
1	**egg**
4	**tablespoons slivered almonds**

Mix all ingredients together. Drop by ½ teaspoon onto sprayed foil paper on cookie sheet. Batter tends to spread so leave plenty of room.

Bake in a preheated 350 degree oven for 10 minutes. Watch carefully so they don't burn. Cool 15 minutes on foil before removing from pan.

These cookies are also wonderful when you dip them in melted chocolate discs. This chocolate can be purchased in a craft store, gourmet cooking store or grocery store. Hold the cookie and dip on one side. I like to see what the cookies look like so I don't cover the whole thing. Put the cookies on wax paper until the chocolate hardens.

CHOCOLATE CHUNK MACADAMIA COOKIES

Yield: 60 small cookies   *Preheat oven to 350 degrees*

Freezes well

2	**cups all purpose flour**
1	**teaspoon soda**
½	**teaspoon salt**
1	**cup (2 sticks) butter or margarine**
¾	**cup brown sugar, packed**
½	**cup granulated sugar**
1	**teaspoon vanilla extract**
1	**egg**
12	**ounces semi sweet chocolate chunks**
8	**ounces or 2 small jars of Macadamia nuts**

Spray cookie sheets with non-stick cooking spray.

In a small bowl combine flour, soda and salt. Set aside. In a large bowl, combine butter, both sugars, and vanilla extract; mix well until creamy. Beat in egg and add flour mixture. Beat well. Stir in chocolate chunks and nuts. Drop by rounded teaspoons about 2 inches apart on the cookie sheet.

Bake in a preheated 350 degree oven for about 8 to 10 minutes. Cool 10 minutes and remove from the cookie sheet.

These cookies can be dipped in melted chocolate discs by holding ½ the cookie and dipping the rest.

For a change of taste, substitute the Macadamia nuts with pecans, walnuts or coconut.

COCOA-BROWNIE COOKIES

Yield: 25-30 cookies   *Preheat oven to 350 degrees*

These cookies are chewy and delicious!

- **3   cups firmly packed brown sugar**
- **7   tablespoons cocoa (I use Droste's)**
- **2   tablespoons flour**
- **3   egg whites**
- **2   cups chopped pecans**
- **Parchment paper**

In a mixer, combine sugar, cocoa and flour until well blended. Add egg whites and beat on high speed for one minute. Reduce speed to low and add nuts. Stir just until blended.

Line cookie sheets with parchment paper. Drop teaspoon-sized cookies onto pan allowing room for cookies to spread. Bake in a preheated 350 degree oven for 15 minutes. Cool on cookie sheets for 3 minutes before removing to wire racks to cool.

DO NOT FREEZE. Store in an airtight container or a zip-lock plastic bag.

MINI PECAN TARTS

Yield: 60 tarts   *Preheat oven to 350 degrees*

Base:
- 1⅓   **cups butter**
- 8   **ounces cream cheese**
- 2⅔   **cups flour**

Filling:
- 2   **large eggs**
- 1½   **cups brown sugar**
- 2   **teaspoons butter, melted**
- 2   **teaspoons vanilla extract**
- 1   **cup chopped pecans**
  confectioners sugar

Let butter and cream cheese soften at room temperature for about 1 hour, then mix well. Add flour and mix until the dough is soft. Chill for 1 hour.

Break off small pieces of dough and press into sprayed mini tins. Use a utensil with a rounded top that's been dusted with flour to spread dough evenly in muffin tins. Bake for 10-12 minutes in a preheated 350 degree oven until dough puffs up.

While the base is baking, prepare the filling. In a mixer, beat eggs and add brown sugar, melted butter, vanilla extract and nuts. Mix well.

Fill the muffin tins ¾ full with filling and return to oven for 15 minutes. Reduce oven to 250 degrees and bake for an additional 20 minutes or until brown. Remove from oven, let cool and then dust with confectioners sugar.

Freezes well.

POTATO CHIP COOKIES

Yield: 50 cookies   *Preheat oven to 350 degrees*

1   **pound butter**
1   **cup sugar**
1   **cup crushed potato chips (I always use Jay's)**
1   **teaspoon vanilla extract**
1   **cup crushed almonds**
1   **tablespoon almond extract**
3   **cups flour**
    confectioners sugar

Cream ingredients in order: butter, sugar, potato chips, vanilla extract, crushed almonds and almond extract. Beat in flour and combine well.

Place by spoonfuls on a sprayed cookie sheet.

Bake in a preheated 350 degree oven for 10 to 12 minutes. Don't let them get too brown. When cool, sprinkle with confectioners sugar.

This recipe freezes well.

CHOCOLATE BON BONS

Yield: 40 cookies   *Preheat oven to 350 degrees*

1	**cup butter**
½	**cup unsifted confectioners sugar**
1	**teaspoon vanilla extract**
2¼	**cups sifted flour**
1	**14 ounce bag Hershey's Kisses**

Cream butter and sugar. Blend in vanilla extract and add flour. Mix until well blended. Break off small pieces of dough and wrap around each Hershey's Kiss until well formed.

Spray cookie sheet with non-stick cooking spray. Place cookies fairly close together. Bake in a preheated 350 degree oven for 10-12 minutes. Sprinkle with confectioners sugar when cool.

P.S. For a change, substitute the Kisses with nuts, baking cherries or chocolate stars.

CHOCOLATE CHIP BUTTER COOKIES

Yield: 40 cookies   *Preheat oven to 350 degrees*

When I was given this recipe I was told not to share it, but it is too good to be kept a secret! Sorry, Beverly!

- ½   **pound unsalted butter**
- ½   **pound soft margarine**
- 1   **teaspoon vanilla extract**
- 1   **cup brown sugar**
- 3   **cups flour**
- 1   **6 ounce package of chocolate chips**
- ¾   **cup chopped pecans**
     confectioners sugar for sprinkling

Cream butter and margarine. Add vanilla extract and brown sugar. Mix well. Add flour, chips and nuts. Blend well. Form dough into balls** and place on cookie sheets sprayed with non-stick cooking spray. Space cookies about a ½ inch apart. Bake in a preheated 350 degree oven for 15-20 minutes until light brown. Remove from oven and cool for ten minutes. Then sprinkle with confectioners sugar.

** For this recipe I use a small melon ball utensil, but you can just roll the dough between the palms of your hand. Also, sometimes I add a little more flour if dough feels too sticky.

CRISP BROWNIE COOKIES

Yield: Approx. 48 small brownies   *Preheat oven to 350 degrees*

- **1   stick butter**
- **1   square unsweetened chocolate**
- **1   egg**
- **¼   teaspoon vanilla extract**
- **½   cup sugar**
- **¼   cup sifted flour**
- **½   cup chopped nuts (walnuts or pecans)**

In a small pan, melt butter and square of chocolate. Remove from heat and beat in egg, vanilla extract and sugar. Add sifted flour and spread in a jelly roll pan sprayed with non-stick cooking spray. The mixture will be thin. Sprinkle with nuts.

Bake in a preheated 350 degree oven for 15 minutes.

Cut into squares immediately. This cookie will crisp as it cools. Store in an airtight container or freeze.

NOTES

NOTES

THE BEST BROWNIES AND BARS

The Best Brownies and Bars

BETTER THAN SEX BROWNIES

Yield: 36 brownies   *Preheat oven to 350 degrees*

I use a packaged fudge brownie mix. But you can use my **Fudgy Rich Brownie** recipe if you like everything from scratch. These brownies are 3 layers thick.

Bottom layer: Bake the brownies in a 9 x 13 pan sprayed with non-stick cooking spray following the package instructions. Cool for at least 1 hour.

Filling:
- ½   cup butter
- 2   cups confectioners sugar
- 1   teaspoon vanilla extract
- 2   tablespoons milk

_____

Cream butter and add confectioners sugar, milk, and vanilla extract. Beat until smooth. Spread mixture over cooled brownie layer. Refrigerate for at least 1 hour until firm.

Topping:
- 6   ounce package semi sweet chocolate chips
- 4   tablespoons butter

_____

Melt chocolate chips and butter - cool until spreading consistency. Spread over chilled filling.

Refrigerate again until the chocolate hardens. Cut into bars.

This recipe freezes well!

FUDGY RICH BROWNIES

Yield: 24-32 brownies   *Preheat oven to 350 degrees*

You can use this brownie recipe as a base for all recipes I've given you or just as a great tasting brownie! My friend Felice introduced me to this recipe.

- 1   **package (8 squares) Baker's Unsweetened Chocolate**
- 1   **cup butter or margarine**
- 5   **eggs**
- 3   **cups sugar**
- 1   **tablespoon vanilla extract**
- 1½   **cups unsifted - all purpose flour**
       optional - nuts or M & M's

Melt chocolate and butter in a sauce pan on very low heat stirring constantly. Cool.

Meanwhile, beat eggs, sugar and vanilla extract in a large mixing bowl on high speed for 10 minutes. Blend in chocolate mixture on low speed. Add flour, beating just to blend. Fold in any optional ingredients or leave them plain.

Spread mixture into a 9 x 13 pan sprayed with non-stick cooking spray. Bake in a preheated 350 degree oven for 35 - 40 minutes. DO NOT OVERBAKE!

Cool and cut into squares.

These brownies are very rich, so you may want to cut them into smaller pieces.

CARAMEL BROWNIES

Yield: 36 Brownies   *Preheat oven to 350 degrees*

I use a packaged brownie mix for this recipe. But, if you want to make the batter from scratch, use the **Fudgy Rich Brownies** recipe.

- **1   package brownie mix**
- **1   bag Kraft caramels**
- **2½   ounces evaporated milk (a little less than ½ cup)**
- **6   ounce package chocolate chips**

In a double boiler melt caramels with evaporated milk. Stir constantly. Prepare brownies according to the directions on package.

Spray a 9 x 13 pan with non-stick cooking spray and pour in ½ of brownie batter. Bake in a preheated 350 degree oven for 6 minutes.

Take baked brownies out of the oven and sprinkle on chocolate chips. Cover chips with melted caramel mixture. Cover with remainder of brownie batter and return to oven for an additional 25 minutes.

Cool completely and then cut into squares.

Freezes well!

ROCKY ROAD BROWNIES

Yield: 36 brownies   *Preheat oven to 350 degrees*

I use a packaged brownie mix for this recipe when I'm in a hurry. Otherwise, I use the recipe for **Fudgy Rich Brownies** when I want to make everything from scratch.

1	**brownie recipe**
3	**cups mini marshmallows**
2	**squares unsweetened chocolate**
4	**tablespoons butter**
½	**cup sugar**
½	**teaspoon vanilla extract**
4	**tablespoons milk**

1. Bake brownies and let cool.

2. Sprinkle top of brownies with mini marshmallows and place in a preheated 350 degree oven for a minute - just to slightly brown the marshmallows. Remove from oven and cool.

3. Prepare frosting by melting chocolate with butter. Remove from heat and beat with sugar, vanilla extract and milk in a mixer until spreading consistency.

4. Let brownies cool completely before cutting. Chill in the refrigerator to speed up the cooling process.

AUNTIE CAROL'S FUDGY WUDGY BROWNIES

Preheat oven to 325 degrees

Carol Connors is my husband's cousin. She's a song writer in Los Angeles. One of her most famous lyrics is the theme from "Rocky". These brownies are worth fighting for!

4	**squares Baker's Unsweetened Chocolate**
½	**cup butter or margarine**
4	**eggs**
2	**cups sugar**
1	**cup sifted flour**
1	**teaspoon vanilla extract**
1	**teaspoon coffee liqueur**
1	**cup walnuts, chopped**
1	**6 ounce bag chocolate chip morsels**
¼	**cup coconut**
¼	**cup small marshmallows**

Melt unsweetened chocolate and butter in a double boiler. Set aside to cool slightly.

In a large bowl beat eggs. Gradually add sugar and beat well. Add flour, vanilla extract and liqueur. Add cooled chocolate mixture and blend well. Stir in nuts and chocolate chip morsels.

Spread in a 9 inch square pan that has been sprayed with non-stick cooking spray. Sprinkle coconut and marshmallows on top and bake in a preheated 325 oven for 25-30 minutes.

Remove from oven and cool thoroughly in pan. Cut into squares and dig in!

GERMAN CARAMEL BROWNIES

Yield: 36 brownies   *Preheat oven to 350 degrees*

1	**14 ounce package caramels**
1	**small can of evaporated milk**
1	**package Pillsbury German Chocolate Cake mix**
¾	**cup butter melted**
1	**cup chopped nuts**
1	**cup chocolate chips**

Melt caramels and ⅓ cup evaporated milk in a heavy pan. Set aside.

Spray a 9 x 13 pan with non-stick cooking spray.

Mix cake mix, butter and nuts together. Add ⅓ cup of evaporated milk. Mix again. Pat ½ of this mixture into pan and bake in a preheated 350 degree oven for 6 minutes. Remove from oven and sprinkle chocolate chips on top and then pour melted caramel mixture over the chips. Take rest of cake mixture and spread over caramel.

Bake for an additional 15-18 minutes. Cool for 30 minutes and then cut into squares.

Freezes well.

PECAN BARS

Yield: 36 bars   Preheat oven to 350 degrees

One day when I was baking for my market, I couldn't decide if I should make pecan tarts or not. That's when I made up this new recipe.

Crust:
- 1 cup butter
- ½ cup sugar
- 2 cups flour

Filling:
- 2 teaspoons melted butter
- 1½ cups brown sugar
- 2 large eggs
- 2 teaspoons vanilla extract
- 1 cup chopped pecans
- confectioners sugar for garnish (optional)

Crust:
Cream butter and sugar. Slowly add flour and blend well. Pat crust into a 10 x 15 jelly-roll pan sprayed with non-stick cooking spray and bake for 15 minutes in a preheated 350 degree oven. Remove from oven.

Filling:
Mix melted butter with brown sugar. Add eggs, vanilla extract and blend well. Add chopped pecans and mix well.

Pour filling over crust and return to oven for 15 minutes or until top is golden. Cool and cut into squares. If desired, sprinkle with confectioners sugar.

Freezes well.

HERSHEY CANDY BAR SQUARES

Yield: 6-7 dozen   *Preheat oven to 350 degrees*

- 1   **cup butter or margarine**
- 1   **cup brown sugar, packed**
- 1   **egg yolk**
- 1   **teaspoon vanilla extract**
- 2   **cups flour**
- ¼   **teaspoon salt (optional)**

Topping:
- 6   **Hershey Bars**
- ½   **cup chopped walnuts or pecans**

Cream butter and brown sugar until fluffy. Add egg yolk and vanilla extract. Slowly, beat in flour and salt until well blended.

Spray a jelly roll pan with non-stick cooking spray. Spread dough to cover pan. Use hands to press dough towards corners and pat down evenly. Bake for 20 to 25 minutes in a preheated 350 degree oven until light, golden brown. Remove dough from oven and place candy bars on hot dough until chocolate is soft and melting. Then spread with a knife until all the dough is covered with melted chocolate. Sprinkle with nuts. Cut into squares while warm.

GLAZED LEMON BARS

Yield: 36 bars   *Preheat oven to 350 degrees*

Crust:
- 2 cups all purpose flour
- ½ cup confectioners sugar
- 1 cup butter or margarine

Filling:
- 4 eggs, slightly beaten
- 2 cups sugar
- ¼ cup flour
- 1 teaspoon baking powder
- ¼ cup bottled lemon juice
- 2 teaspoons lemon extract (For more "zip", use 1 tablespoon of lemon extract)

Frosting:
- 1 cup confectioners sugar
- 2-3 tablespoons lemon juice (depending on how tart you like it)
- ¼ cup lemon rind (optional)

Spray a 9 x 13 pan with non-stick cooking spray.

Crust:

In a large bowl combine flour, confectioners sugar and butter at low speed until crumbly. Press into 9 x 13 pan.

Bake in a preheated 350 degree oven for 20 minutes or until light brown.

Filling:

In a large bowl combine eggs, sugar, flour and baking powder. Blend well. Stir in lemon juice and lemon extract. Pour mixture over warm crust.

Return to oven and bake about 25 minutes or until top is light golden brown. Cool completely.

Frosting:

In a small bowl combine confectioners sugar, lemon juice and rind. Blend until smooth. Spread over cooled layer. Cut into bars.

Refrigerate.

LAST MINUTE BARS

Yield: 36 bars   *Preheat oven to 350 degrees*

This recipe works whenever I need a quick, good cookie bar.

Base:
- ½   **cup butter**
- 1¼ **cups graham cracker crumbs**
- 1   **6 ounce package chocolate chips**
- 1   **6 ounce package butterscotch chips**
- 1   **can coconut (3 ounces)**
- 1   **can Eagle Brand Condensed Sweetened milk**

Melt butter in 9 x 13 pan in oven. Add graham cracker crumbs and mix well. Press mixture evenly down in pan to form a crust. Sprinkle both chips over crust. Sprinkle coconut over chips. Punch two holes in top of can of milk on opposite sides and slowly pour evenly over all ingredients.

Bake in a preheated 350 degree oven for 25 minutes. (Coconut and milk should turn light brown.)

Cool 15 minutes before cutting into squares.

P.S. You can also add chopped walnuts or pecans after the chocolate chip layer.

YUMMY RASPBERRY BARS

Yield: 36 bars   *Preheat oven to 350 degrees*

Crust:
- 2 cups flour
- ½ cup sugar
- Pinch of salt (optional)
- 1 cup butter

- 1 cup raspberry preserves

Topping:
- 1½ cups packed brown sugar
- 3 large eggs
- ½ teaspoon vanilla extract
- ½ cup chopped walnuts
- ¾ cups flaked coconut
- 4½ tablespoons flour
- ¾ teaspoon baking powder
- confectioners sugar (optional)

Beat all "crust" ingredients together until crumbly. A good method is to mix flour, sugar and salt. Cut up the frozen butter in 1 tablespoon portions. Put in food processor and turn on/off until crumbly. Pat dough mixture into sprayed jelly roll pan and bake until light brown for 15 to 18 minutes in a preheated 350 degree oven.

Cool crust about 15 minutes and spread 1 cup of raspberry preserves over warm crust. Reduce oven to 325 degrees.

Topping:
On high speed, beat brown sugar, eggs and vanilla extract in a large mixing bowl for 2 to 4 minutes. The mixture should be fluffy. Add walnuts, coconut, flour and baking powder. Stir until batter is well blended. Spread topping over preserves.

Bake about 25-30 minutes until top is brown and center is firm. Cut warm bars in 1½ - 2 inch squares. To increase the number of bars, the squares can then be recut on a diagonal, to create triangular pieces.

Sprinkle with confectioners sugar (optional).

ESTHER'S STRUDEL

Yield: 40 pieces   *Preheat oven to 350 degrees*

I got this recipe from my editor's mother. It's delicious!

Dough
2	sticks butter or margarine, softened
8	ounces sour cream
2¼	cups all purpose flour

Filling
2	large jars apricot preserves (36 ounces)
2	cups chopped walnuts
2½	cups white raisins
	confectioners sugar

Cream butter or margarine in mixer. Alternate adding small amounts of sour cream, then flour, until it becomes too heavy to keep mixing. Add remaining flour with a spoon, or by hand. Dough will be sticky.

Divide into 4 parts and wrap each part in wax paper. Refrigerate overnight.

Remove dough from refrigerator and let soften.

Roll dough out on floured board. It should be as thin as possible and shaped into a rectangle. Spread generously with apricot preserves (not jelly), followed by a sprinkling of chopped walnuts and white raisins. Tightly roll and fold ends under. Place all 4 rolls side by side on a large jelly roll pan which has been well greased.

Bake 1 hour in a preheated 350 degree oven until light golden brown. Cut while warm in 1 inch slices. Cool on pan. Stores well in tin cans. Freezes well.

Sprinkle with confectioners sugar before serving.

ZESTY LEMON BARS

Yield: 36 bars   *Preheat oven to 350 degrees*

Crust:
- 1   **cup butter**
- 2   **cups flour**
- ½   **cup confectioners sugar**

Topping:
- 4   **eggs**
- 2   **cups sugar**
- 4   **tablespoons flour**
- 1   **teaspoon baking powder**
- 4   **tablespoons lemon juice**
- 1   **tablespoon lemon extract**
- 1   **tablespoon grated lemon rind (optional)**
      confectioners sugar

Crust:
Beat butter and add flour and sugar. Press into a sprayed jelly roll pan. Bake for 15 minutes in a preheated 350 degree oven.

Topping:
On medium speed beat eggs and sugar. Add flour, baking powder, lemon juice, lemon extract, and lemon rind. Beat for 2 minutes and pour evenly over hot crust. Return to oven and bake for another 25 minutes. When cool, sprinkle with confectioners sugar and cut into squares.

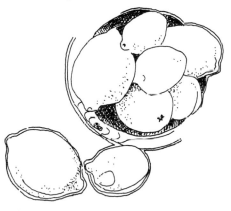

SIX LAYER FRUITY STRUDEL

Preheat oven to 350 degrees

Dough:
2¾ cups flour
1 teaspoon baking powder
1 teaspoon baking soda
2 tablespoons water
6 eggs separated, reserve 2 of the egg whites
½ cup vegetable oil
2 orange rinds, grated
1 lemon rind, grated

Filling:
1 cup nuts, finely chopped
1 teaspoon cinnamon
1 cup sugar
1 cup white raisins
2 cups apricot preserves (optional — strawberry or blueberry)

Mix dough ingredients together and divide into 6 balls. Roll out first ball to fit a 9 x 13 pan sprayed with non-stick cooking spray. Place on bottom.

To prepare filling, combine all ingredients except for preserves.

Sprinkle dough with filling and dot with preserves. Put second layer of dough on top and repeat process. Reserve a small amount of filling to use as garnish.

Bake in a preheated 350 degree oven for 20 minutes.

Remove from oven and glaze with remaining egg white that have been whipped. Sprinkle rest of sugar mixture on top. Bake 20 minutes more.

Cool 20 minutes and cut into squares.

MY MOTHER'S MANDEL BREAD

Yield: about 60 pieces   *Preheat oven to 350 degrees*

My mother was always asked to bring this recipe whenever people invited her over.

- 1 **cup butter**
- 1 **cup sugar**
- 4 **eggs**
- 1/8 **teaspoon salt (optional)**
- 1 **teaspoon vanilla extract**
- 4 **cups flour, sifted**
- 1 **teaspoon baking powder**
- 1 **cup nuts, chopped — walnuts or pecans**
- 1 **teaspoon cinnamon**

Cream butter and sugar. Add eggs, salt and vanilla extract. Add the sifted flour, baking powder and chopped nuts. Blend well.

Divide dough into 4 parts. Shape dough into long loaves on cookie sheets sprayed with non-stick cooking spray. Bake in a preheated 350 degree oven until light brown, about 30 - 35 minutes. Remove from oven and cut into 1/2 inch slices. Lay slices on side and put back in oven for a few more minutes to brown. Combine cinnamon and sugar. Sprinkle while warm.

Freezes well.

ICE CREAM MANDEL BREAD

Yield: 48 pieces   *Preheat oven to 350 degrees*

Thanks, Lori!

Dough:
  1   **pint vanilla ice cream (I use Hagen Daz), softened***
  1   **pound margarine, softened**
  4   **cups flour**

Filling:
  1   **small jar apricot jam**
  1   **small jar raspberry jam**
  1   **box white raisins**
  1   **3 ounce container sugar/cinnamon**
      Confectioners sugar for decoration (optional)

In a mixer, beat ice cream, margarine and flour. Mix well and knead briefly. Chill overnight or several hours in a wax paper covered bowl. Divide dough into 8 balls. Roll out into rectangle forms on a lightly floured surface. (Flour the rolling pin because the dough is sticky.) On the rolled out dough, spread a layer of jam. (Use one flavor per roll.) Cover jam with raisins and then sprinkle on a layer of cinnamon and sugar. Roll up like a jelly roll and tuck ends under.

Place on cookie sheets sprayed with non-stick cooking spray. Bake in a preheated 350 degree oven for 45 minutes. Cut while warm.

When cool, sprinkle with confectioners sugar.

The dough can be made ahead and frozen. The completed mandel bread freezes well!

* For those on a restricted diet, tofu can be substituted.

NOTES

NOTES

MY FAVORITE CAKES AND PIES

My Favorite Cakes and Pies

SO YOU WANT TO BAKE YOUR OWN PIE CRUST . . .

1½   cups sifted flour
½   teaspoon salt
½   cup shortening
4-5   tablespoons cold water

Sift flour and salt. Cut in shortening until crumbly. Sprinkle water over crumbs a little at a time and mix after each addition until dough can be formed into a ball.

Lightly flour a surface and roll out ball to size of pie plate. Fold dough in quarters and then place in center of plate. Unfold and gently pat to the form of the pan. Remove any excess on the edges.

For a double crust:

2   cups flour
1   teaspoon salt
⅔   cup shortening
5-7   tablespoons cold water

Divide dough into 2 balls and follow above directions.

CHOCOLATE CHIP PIE

Preheat oven to 325 degrees

My friend Margie gave me this recipe. This is a special dessert if you want to impress your company.

2	**eggs**
½	**cup flour**
½	**cup sugar**
½	**cup firmly packed brown sugar**
1	**cup butter, melted and cooled to room temperature**
6	**ounce package semi sweet chocolate chips**
1	**cup chopped walnuts**
1	**9 inch unbaked pie shell**

In a large bowl beat eggs until foamy. Beat in flour, sugar, and brown sugar until well blended. Blend in melted butter. Stir in chocolate chips and walnuts. Pour batter into a pie shell.

Bake 1 hour. Remove from oven and serve warm. This pie is delicious served with ice cream or whipped cream.

This pie freezes well.

MY BEST APPLE PIE

Preheat oven to 350 degrees

My parents used to bring me a bushel of apples every year from their trees. So what did I do? I baked apple pies to last the whole year.

- **2**   **frozen or refrigerated pie shells**
- **6**   **baking apples, peeled and sliced**
- **¾**   **cup sugar**
- **2**   **tablespoons all-purpose flour**
- **½**   **teaspoon cinnamon**
-     **dash nutmeg**
- **2**   **tablespoons butter**

Mix together the sliced apples, sugar, flour, cinnamon, and nutmeg. Pour into a prepared pie shell. Dot top of apples with butter and cover with second pie shell. Pinch top and bottom crusts together so they totally cover the pie. Make small slits on top of pastry to make sure the pie bakes thoroughly.

Bake in a preheated 350 degree oven for 1 hour or until crust is light brown.

P.S. This pie is delicious served warm with ice cream. When in season, peaches make a fabulous substitute.

QUICK & EASY BANANA CREAM PIE

1   graham cracker crust
2   bananas
1   pint vanilla ice cream
1   cup milk
1   banana instant pudding

Slice bananas and cover the bottom of a graham cracker crust. Whip ice cream, milk and instant pudding together. Pour mixture over bananas and chill until set.

Serve and enjoy.

YUMMY COCONUT CREAM PIE

Barry's Aunt Edith was known for this special pie. As a child it was his favorite pie and he still loves it today.

Bake 1 pie shell and let cool until ready to use.

Filling:
- 3/4 **cup sugar**
- 4 **tablespoons cornstarch**
- 1/4 **teaspoon salt**
- 3 **eggs separated**
- 2 **cups milk, scalded**
- 1 **tablespoon butter**
- 1 **teaspoon vanilla extract**
- 1 **can coconut**

In a medium saucepan mix together 1/2 cup sugar, cornstarch and salt. Add egg yolks and mix in 2 tablespoons of scalded milk. Blend well. Add rest of milk and beat until smooth. Cook over low heat until thick. Beat in butter and vanilla extract. Remove from heat.

Take 1/4 can of coconut and sprinkle some on bottom of pie crust. Add 1/4 of coconut to batter and stir. Pour 1/2 batter into pie shell. Take another 1/4 can of coconut and sprinkle on top of filling. Then add remainder of filling to pie shell, reserving balance of coconut for topping.

To prepare topping whip egg whites and 1/4 cup sugar together until they form peaks. Cover pie with meringue topping and sprinkle remaining coconut on top.

Bake in a preheated 350 degree oven for about 20 minutes or until meringue is browned.

CHOCOLATE PECAN PIE

Preheat oven to 350 degrees

This pie tastes great warm! As an extra treat, serve it with ice cream or whipped cream. Delish!

1	**unbaked pie shell**
3	**eggs**
1	**cup Karo light or dark corn syrup**
1	**package (4 ounces) Baker's German Sweet Chocolate or 4 squares semi-sweet chocolate, melted and cooled**
1/3	**cup sugar**
2	**tablespoons butter, melted**
1	**teaspoon vanilla extract**
1½	**cups pecan halves**

In a large bowl, mix eggs, corn syrup, melted and cooled chocolate, sugar, melted butter and vanilla extract. Stir until well blended. Fold in pecans.

Pour into pastry shell and bake in a preheated 350 degree oven for 50-60 minutes until set.

Freezes well!

PIZZA FRUIT DELIGHT

Preheat oven to 350 degrees

This recipe is great on a hot summer day. It looks cool and refreshing and tastes delicious!

1	**14 inch pizza pan**

Crust:

1	**cup butter**
½	**cup sugar**
½	**cup packed brown sugar**
1	**egg**
1	**teaspoon vanilla extract**
1¾	**cup flour**

1	**8 ounce cream cheese, whipped in a mixer**
2	**cans sliced peaches**
1	**pint strawberries**
20	**green grapes**
1	**pint blueberries**
1	**8 ounce Cool Whip**

To make crust, in a large bowl beat butter, add sugar and brown sugar and beat until fluffy. Add egg and vanilla extract and beat well. Add flour on low speed and blend well. Spread the dough evenly onto a sprayed 14 inch pizza pan.

Bake crust in a preheated 350 degree oven for about 12 minutes until golden brown. When cool, lightly spread crust with whipped cream cheese. Pat dry sliced peaches and arrange on top of the cream cheese. Place grapes, sliced strawberries, and blueberries on top. You can arrange the fruit in a wedge style to resemble a cut up pizza or just place to fill entire pizza. You do not have to use all the blueberries or all the strawberries.

Dollop a little whipped topping for decoration. Cut and enjoy.

Pizza dough, without topping, may be frozen.

* All other seasonal fresh fruits can be used. If using bananas, serve immediately because they turn brown.

JASON'S FAVORITE CHOCOLATE PISTACHIO CAKE

Preheat oven to 350 degrees

This is my son's favorite cake! I've been making it especially for him for at least 12 years.

Mix together:

1	**package white or yellow cake mix**
4	**eggs**
¾	**cup oil**
1	**cup sour cream**
1	**package instant pistachio pudding**
1	**5½ ounce Hershey's Chocolate Syrup**
	confectioners sugar

Mix all ingredients except syrup, with an electric beater on medium. Pour ¾ of mixture into a greased or sprayed bundt pan. Add syrup to remaining batter. Mix well and pour on top of batter in bundt pan. Take a knife and run it through batter using a swirling motion. This will marbleize the batter.

Bake in a preheated 350 degree oven for 50-60 minutes. Check for doneness with a toothpick. Remove from oven and cool for 1 hour. Turn onto a plate and sprinkle with confectioners sugar.

LIZZY'S LEMON SURPRISE CAKE

My daughter Lizzy makes this cake for me at market time. The surprise is that it's easy! This recipe comes from our friend Susie.

   2   **cans lemon custard (Thank You brand)**
   2   **packages lady fingers**
   1   **8 ounce Cool Whip**
   1   **pint fresh strawberries, sliced**

Spray a 9 inch springform pan with non-stick cooking spray.

Place lady fingers on bottom of springform and stand them up next to each other to line inside border of pan. Pour 1 can of lemon custard on top of the lady fingers, then add ½ container of Cool Whip, sliced strawberries to cover Cool Whip and then add another layer of lady fingers. Repeat lemon and Cool Whip with strawberries being top layer.

Chill at least 2 hours. Unmold and serve.

Looks great and tastes fantastic!

SOUR CREAM COFFEE CAKE

Preheat oven to 350 degrees

This recipe was requested by the Chicago Sun Times.

2	**sticks unsalted butter**
2¼	**cups sugar**
2	**eggs beaten**
2	**cups sour cream**
1	**tablespoon vanilla extract**
2	**cups all purpose flour**
1	**tablespoon baking powder**
½	**cup chopped pecans**
2	**teaspoons cinnamon**

Cream together butter and 2 cups of sugar (reserving ¼ cup of sugar). Add eggs and blend well. Add sour cream and vanilla extract.

Sift flour and baking powder. Add to creamed mixture, beat until blended.
DO NOT OVER BEAT!

In a separate bowl mix ¼ cup sugar with pecans and cinnamon.

Spray bundt pan with non-stick cooking spray. Pour ½ of dough mixture into bundt pan. Sprinkle with ¾ of the cinnamon, sugar and nut mixture. Reserve ¼ of sugar mixture to top cake. Add remaining batter and top with sugar mixture.

Bake in a preheated 350 degree oven for 1 hour. Cool for 1 hour before unmolding.

This cake is incredibly moist and freezes well.

BAKED MERINGUE SPICED CAKE

Preheat oven to 350 degrees

2²/₃	cups cake flour
1	teaspoon ground cloves
1	teaspoon baking powder
1	teaspoon baking soda
1	teaspoon cinnamon
½	pound butter
2	cups brown sugar, packed
2	eggs + 2 egg yolks, beaten
1	cup sour milk
	(To make sour milk, add 1 tablespoon vinegar to regular milk. Let sit about 1 hour.)

Meringue:

2	egg whites
1	cup brown sugar
½	cup chopped nuts

Sift flour, ground cloves, baking powder, baking soda, and cinnamon 3 times. Set aside.

Cream butter and sugar until fluffy. Add beaten eggs and yolks. Beat thoroughly. Add sifted dry ingredients, alternating with milk.

Pour into a 9 x 13 pan sprayed with non-stick cooking spray.

To make meringue use a small, clean, dry bowl. Put in egg whites and beat on high speed. When foamy, slowly begin to add brown sugar and beat until peaks begin to form. Do not over process. Stir in nuts. Spread meringue on top of cake and bake in a preheated 350 degree oven for about 1 hour. Let cool before cutting.

JACKIE'S COFFEE CAKE

Preheat oven to 325 degrees

At market time, my friend Jackie makes this cake for me. It's a real treat!

- ½ **cup butter**
- 1 **cup sugar**
- 2 **eggs**
- 2 **cups all purpose flour**
- 1 **teaspoon baking soda**
- 1 **teaspoon baking powder**
- ½ **teaspoon salt**
- 1 **cup sour cream**
- 1 **teaspoon vanilla extract**
- ⅓ **cup brown sugar**
- ¼ **cup sugar**
- 1 **teaspoon cinnamon**

Cream butter until soft. Add sugar, and cream until light & fluffy. Add eggs one at a time and beat well. Sift together flour, baking soda, baking powder, and salt and add to the creamed mixture. Stir in sour cream and vanilla extract. Mix well.

In a separate bowl, prepare topping by combining brown sugar, sugar, and cinnamon.

Pour ½ batter into a 9 x 13 pan sprayed with non-stick cooking spray. Cover with ¾ topping mixture. Pour on the remaining batter and sprinkle on remaining topping.

Bake for 40 minutes in a preheated 325 degree oven. Let cool before cutting into squares.

This cake freezes well.

BETTER THAN CHOCOLATE CAKE

Preheat oven to 350 degrees

1	box yellow cake mix
1	box instant vanilla pudding
½	cup vegetable oil
½	cup water
4	eggs (one at a time)
1	cup sour cream
1	bar grated German chocolate
1	6 ounce package chocolate chips
1	6 ounce package butterscotch chips
½	cup chopped pecans

On medium speed, combine cake mix, pudding, oil and water until blended. Add eggs, one at a time, and blend well. Add sour cream and mix again.

By hand, fold in grated German chocolate, chocolate chips, butterscotch chips and chopped pecans. Spray a bundt pan with non-stick cooking spray and pour in the batter.

Bake in a preheated 350 degree oven for 1 hour. Cool for 1 hour before removing from pan.

Freezes well.

CHOCOLATE CHIP CAKE

Preheat oven to 350 degrees

¼ **pound sweet butter**
1 **cup sugar**
2 **eggs**
2 **cups sifted cake flour**
1 **teaspoon baking powder**
1 **teaspoon baking soda**
½ **pint sour cream**
1 **teaspoon vanilla extract**
6 **ounces semi sweet chocolate chips**
   confectioners sugar

Spray a bundt pan with non-stick cooking spray. Set aside.

In a mixer, cream together butter, sugar and eggs. Add sifted cake flour, baking powder and baking soda. Add sour cream and vanilla extract. Blend in chocolate chips.

Pour batter into a bundt pan sprayed with non-stick cooking spray and bake for 40 minutes in a preheated 350 degree oven. Test for doneness with a toothpick and continue baking up to 1 hour, if necessary. Cool for 1 hour and unmold. Sprinkle with confectioners sugar.

Freezes well.

AUNT FANNY'S NUT CAKE

This cake is a family favorite any time of the year!

10	**eggs, separated, room temperature**
1¾	**cups sugar**
¾	**cup orange juice**
1	**cup matzo meal**
1	**cup nuts, ground**

Mix yolks with 1 cup sugar. Add orange juice, matzo meal and nuts. Blend well. In a separate bowl, beat egg whites until soft peaks start to form. Slowly add ¾ cup sugar and beat until stiff, but not dry. Fold in egg yolk mixture.

Pour batter into a greased tube pan. Bake for 1 hour and 10 minutes in a preheated 350 degree oven.

BLUEBERRY COFFEE CAKE

Preheat oven to 350 degrees

This coffee cake tastes like a cheese torte.

Cake:
- 1½ cups flour
- ½ cup sugar
- ½ cup butter
- 1½ teaspoons baking powder
- 1 egg
- 1 teaspoon vanilla extract
- 1 quart blueberries

Topping:
- 2 cups sour cream
- 1 egg
- ½ cup sugar
- 1 teaspoon vanilla extract

1. Combine all ingredients for cake except blueberries. Mix well.

2. Pat into a 9 inch or 10 inch springform pan sprayed with non-stick cooking spray.

3. Sprinkle berries over the dough.

4. Combine ingredients for topping and mix well.

5. Pour topping over blueberries.

Bake in a preheated 350 degree oven for 1 hour or until edge of custard is lightly browned. Cool 1 hour before removing from pan.

Freezes well.

CARROT CAKE

Preheat oven to 350 degrees

Cake:
- 1½ **cups butter**
- 2 **cups sugar**
- 4 **eggs**
- 2 **cups flour**
- 1 **heaping teaspoon cinnamon**
- 2 **teaspoons baking soda**
- 3 **cups packed shredded carrots with liquid**
- 1 **teaspoon vanilla extract**
- ½ **cup walnuts or pecans (optional)**

Frosting:
- 6 **ounces cream cheese, softened**
- 1 **cup butter, softened**
- 1 **16 ounce box confectioners sugar**
- 2 **teaspooons vanilla extract**

Cream butter and sugar. Add eggs and blend well. Sift flour, cinnamon and baking soda and add to batter. Add shredded carrots, vanilla extract and nuts.

Spray 2 round cake pans or 2 square 8 inch cake pans with non-stick cooking spray. Pour in batter and make sure it is evenly distributed. Bake in a preheated 350 degree oven for 45 minutes. The cakes will rise and then sink in center, so be sure to have enough batter in center.

Cool for 1 hour and frost between the layers and on top.

This cake freezes well even with frosting.

To make frosting, mix cream cheese and butter. Slowly add confectioners sugar and beat until well blended. Add vanilla extract and stir until spreading consistency.

CHOCOLATE ENGLISH TRIFLE

Easy to prepare, impressive to serve!

1   **chocolate cake (I bake a Duncan Hines Chocolate Fudge Cake in a 9 x 13 pan)**
2   **packages of chocolate pudding, prepared or 2 cans Thank You brand chocolate pudding**
1   **can (small) Hershey's Syrup**
4   **large bananas**
½   **cup chopped walnuts (optional)**
1   **12 ounce Cool Whip**
1   **Hershey Bar (shaved) or 1-6 ounce bag of mini-chocolate chips**

1. Cut cake in half. Take half and cut into chunk pieces to cover bottom of glass bowl.

2. Cover with one can of pudding.

3. Drizzle ½ can of syrup on top of pudding layer.

4. Cover pudding layer with ½ of the sliced bananas and nuts.

5. Top with ½ of Cool Whip. Repeat the sequence beginning with chunks of cake and continue through the layer of Cool Whip. Sprinkle with the shavings of the Hershey bar or mini-chocolate chips.

This recipe is also great using banana cake, bananas, vanilla pudding and strawberries. Do not use Hershey's Syrup for this version.

COOKIE SHEET APPLE CAKE OR PLUM CAKE

Preheat oven to 350 degrees

This cake is made in a cookie sheet with sides. When prune plums are in season, I use them instead of the apples and it tastes like a plum kuchen.

2   **sticks butter**
1   **cup sugar**
2   **cups flour**
1   **egg**
    shot of bourbon (optional)
    72 slices of apple (or . . . 48 tiny prune plums cut in half. If using larger plums, cut in half and then into slices.)
    confectioners sugar for sprinkling on finished cake
    whip cream or Cool Whip for garnish

Mix butter, sugar, flour, egg and bourbon together and place in refrigerator for 1 hour. While that is chilling, split the plums and pit them or slice the apples. (P.S. If you are using small apples you'll need more apple slices.)

Pat dough into a cookie sheet with sides that is sprayed with non-stick cooking spray. Place apples or plums on top and line them in rows until all the dough is covered.

Bake in a preheated 350 degree oven until dough turns golden, approximately 30 minutes. When cool, sprinkle with confectioners sugar. Cut into squares and serve with whipped cream or Cool Whip on the side.

When in season, sliced fresh peaches are a delicious substitute.

Freezes well.

P.S. To make this a little fancier, melt 6 ounces of apricot preserves over low heat and cool slightly. Brush over the fruit slices. As an optional garnish, chop up pistachio nuts and sprinkle lightly down the center of each row, then bake according to the directions. **DO NOT FREEZE** with the above additions.

DONNA'S ICE CREAM SUNDAE CAKE

A refreshing dessert that kids and adults love.

40	**Oreo or Hydrox cookies**
¾	**stick butter, melted**
½	**gallon ice cream, any flavor, softened**
1	**pound jar Smucker's Fudge Sauce**
1	**cup nuts (optional)**

1. Crush cookies and stir together with melted butter.

2. Pat ¾ of crumbs into the 9 x 13 pan sprayed with non-stick cooking spray

   (Reserve ¼ of crumbs for topping.)

3. Pour softened ice cream on top of crumbs.

4. Freeze for 3 hours.

5. Pour fudge sauce over ice cream.

6. Sprinkle nuts over the entire cake.

7. Sprinkle extra crumbs over fudge and place back in freezer for another 45 minutes.

8. Remove from freezer a few minutes before serving.

9. Cut into squares as you serve.

HEATH BAR ICE CREAM CAKE

3 packages lady fingers
6 pints vanilla ice cream
9 small Heath Bars, crushed
6 teaspoons instant coffee
½ pint heavy whipping cream
¼ cup confectioners sugar
2 tablespoons cocoa
1 can fudge sauce (optional)

This is made in a 8 or 9 inch springform pan sprayed with non-stick cooking spray.

In a large bowl, soften ice cream. Sprinkle with instant coffee and crushed Heath bars. Mix well. Line sides and bottom of prepared spring form pan with lady fingers. Pour ½ of ice cream mixture on lady fingers. Add another layer of lady fingers on top of ice cream. Pour on the remaining ice cream.

Prepare topping by whipping up heavy cream with confectioners sugar and cocoa. Frost top of cake and put in freezer to harden.

Take cake out of freezer a few minutes before serving. Remove sides of springform pan and serve with the fudge sauce on the side!

This is a beautiful, delicious treat!

COOKIES AND CREAM CHEESECAKE

Preheat oven to 350 degrees

I "dreamed" up this recipe one night when I couldn't sleep!

1	box plain chocolate wafers, ground
⅓	cup butter, melted
1¼	cup sugar
3	8 ounce packages of cream cheese, softened
2	teaspoons vanilla extract
3	eggs
6	Oreo cookies, ground
1	cup sour cream

To prepare crust, chop chocolate wafers into small crumbs. Add melted butter and ¼ cup of sugar. Mix well and press into the bottom of a 8 or 9 inch spring form pan sprayed with non-stick cooking spray.

In a mixer beat cream cheese until fluffy. Add 1 cup sugar and vanilla extract. Beat in eggs, one at a time. Add ¾ of the Oreo cookie crumbs and stir until well blended. Add sour cream and mix well.

Pour over prepared crust and sprinkle top with remaining ¼ of Oreo cookie crumbs. Bake in a preheated 350 degree oven for 60-70 minutes. Turn off oven and leave cake in for an additional hour with the oven door ajar.

Remove from oven and cool for at least four hours or overnight. Remove side and serve or freeze.

P.S. A variation to this recipe is to double my "Shiny Chocolate Glaze" and spread it over the top and sides of the cooled cake. Then take 6 - 8 whole Oreo cookies and gently push them, standing on their sides, along the border of the top so most of the cookie is showing. This makes a very elegant presentation.

SHINY CHOCOLATE GLAZE

This recipe is used for regular cakes, brownies, and it's great on some of the cheese cake recipes you will find throughout the book.

½ **cup chocolate chips**
2 **tablespoons butter**
2 **tablespoons corn syrup**

In a small saucepan, melt the chocolate chips, butter and corn syrup over low heat. When melted, spread over the cooled cake.

P.S. If you are covering a cheese cake, double the recipe.

LOUIS DELL'OLIO'S CHOCOLATE CHIP CHEESECAKE

★ ★ ★ ★ ★ ★ ★ ★ ★ ★ ★ ★ ★ ★ ★ ★ ★ ★

Preheat oven to 350 degrees

Louis Dell'Olio is the highly respected designer for Anne Klein and Company. His sleek and sophisticated modern classics are the favorites of women all over the country. You'll love the "design" of this cheesecake!

Cake:

1½	cups flour
1	cup sugar
¼	cup cocoa
1	teaspoon baking soda
½	teaspoon salt
1	cup water
½	cup vegetable oil
1	teaspoon vinegar
1	teaspoon vanilla extract

Topping:

1	8 ounce package cream cheese, softened
1	3 ounce package cream cheese, softened
1	egg
½	cup sugar
⅛	teaspoon salt
6	ounces semi-sweet chocolate chips

To make cake, blend all ingredients together. Batter may appear thin. Pour into 8 inch square pan that has been sprayed generously with non-stick cooking spray.

To make topping, mix cream cheese, egg, sugar and salt. Beat until well blended. Stir in chocolate chips. Drop by teaspoonfuls over cake layer and spread evenly.

Bake in a preheated 350 degree oven for 50 minutes. Cool and cut into squares.

WORLD'S BEST CHEESECAKE

Preheat oven to 350 degrees

I use this basic recipe for all my special, creamy cheesecakes.

1¾	**cups graham cracker crumbs**
⅓	**cup butter, melted**
1¼	**cups sugar**
3	**8 ounce packages of cream cheese**
2	**teaspoons vanilla extract**
3	**eggs**
1	**cup sour cream**

Spray an 8 or 9 inch springform with non-stick cooking spray. Set aside.

To form the crust, blend graham cracker crumbs with melted butter and ¼ cup sugar. Press firmly into the prepared spring form.

In a mixer beat cream cheese until fluffy. Add 1 cup sugar and the vanilla extract. Beat in eggs, one at a time. Blend in sour cream.

Pour over prepared crust and bake for 60-70 minutes in a preheated 350 degree oven until firm then turn off oven and leave door ajar for an additional hour. Remove cake from oven and cool. Chill at least 4 hours or overnight in the refrigerator. Remove from springform and serve or freeze until needed.

P.S. This makes a fabulous, plain cheesecake. To make it fancier, top the cake with a can of your favorite fruit pie filling. Personally I use cherry or blueberry. The cake looks beautiful and tastes great!

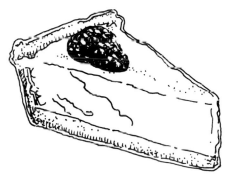

PEANUT BUTTER CUP CHEESECAKE

Preheat oven to 350 degrees

This recipe is another one of my nighttime inspirations.

1	**box chocolate wafer cookies, ground into crumbs**
1/3	**cup butter, melted**
1 1/4	**cups sugar**
3	**8 ounce packages cream cheese, softened**
2	**teaspoons vanilla extract**
3	**eggs**
1/4	**cup peanut butter**
1	**cup sour cream**
8	**mini chocolate peanut butter cups (for garnish)**

Glaze:

1/2	**cup chocolate chips**
2	**tablespoons butter**
2	**tablespoons corn syrup**

To form crust, blend chocolate wafer crumbs, melted butter and 1/4 cup sugar. Press mixture into an 8 or 9 inch springform pan sprayed with non-stick cooking spray.

In a mixer, beat cream cheese until fluffy. Add 1 cup sugar and vanilla extract. Beat in eggs one at a time. Add the peanut butter and sour cream. Blend well.

Pour batter into prepared pan and bake in a preheated 350 degree oven for 60-70 minutes. Leave cake in oven with door ajar an additional hour. Remove from oven and cool. Chill for at least 4 hours or overnight.

To prepare glaze, melt chocolate chips, butter and corn syrup in a small sauce pan on low heat. Remove sides of the springform and spread chocolate mixture on top of cheesecake. Place the peanut butter cups around the top of the cake in a circle with a little space between each.

This cake freezes well and is a dream for peanut butter lovers!

P.S. If you want to glaze the whole cake, double the recipe; and for additional beauty, stick a few more peanut butter cups on the side.

CREAM CHEESE CHERRY CUP CAKES

Yield: 24   *Preheat oven to 350 degrees*

- ¼ **cup butter, melted**
- 1 **cup graham cracker crumbs**
- 1 **8 ounce cream cheese, softened**
- ¼ **cup sugar**
- 1 **egg**
- 1 **can cherry pie filling**

Melt butter and blend with graham cracker crumbs. Line mini muffin tins with paper cups, or spray with non-stick cooking spray.

Using a teaspoon, press a small amount of the crumb mixture into each cup.

In a mixer, blend cream cheese, sugar and egg until smooth. Spread this mixture over the crust until the cups are ³/₄'s full. Top with cherry pie filling and bake in a preheated 350 degree oven for 10 minutes.

Remove from oven and cool in the refrigerator for at least 1 hour before serving.

This recipe freezes well!

PLUM DUMP CAKE

When a friend of mine gave me a piece of this cake to taste I couldn't believe that it was made with baby food. This cake is called a dump cake because you "dump" all the ingredients together and bake!

Cake:
- 3 eggs
- 2 cups sugar
- 2 cups flour
- 1 cup oil
- 1 teaspoon cinnamon
- Dash of ground cloves
- 3 teaspoons baking powder
- 1 cup chopped nuts (pecans or walnuts)
- 2 small jars of strained plum baby food.

Glaze:
- 1 cup confectioners sugar
- juice of one lemon

Mix all the cake ingredients together and pour into a sprayed bundt pan. Bake for 1 hour in a preheated 350 degree oven. Cool for 1 hour. Remove cake from pan.

To prepare glaze, mix confectioners sugar with juice. The glaze should be thick enough to drizzle. Use lemon juice to adjust thickness. Put in a measuring cup with spout and drizzle over cake.

SARAH'S POUND CAKE

Preheat oven to 325 degrees

This is a market favorite! It is wonderful marbleized with chocolate! You get two cakes from this recipe.

1	**pound butter or margarine**
1	**pound confectioners sugar**
6	**eggs**
3	**cups sifted cake flour**
1½-2	**tablespoons vanilla extract**
2	**squares unsweetened chocolate, melted (optional) or 2 prepared packages of melted chocolate**

Cream butter and slowly add confectioners sugar. Drop in eggs, one at a time, until light and fluffy. Add sifted cake flour and vanilla extract. Continue to mix until well blended. Divide batter into 2 loaf pans. To marbleize cake, melt squares of chocolate and pour equally on top of batter. With a knife, cut through batter with a swirling motion.

Bake in a preheated 325 degree oven for 1 hour and 20 minutes. Let stand 5 minutes and then invert.

Freezes well.

SOUR CREAM CAKE

Preheat oven to 350 degrees

Cake:
- ½   **pound butter**
- 1   **cup sugar**
- 3   **eggs**
- 2½   **cups all purpose flour, sifted**
- 3   **teaspoons baking powder**
- 1   **teaspoon baking soda**
- 1   **cup sour cream**
- 1   **teaspoon vanilla extract**

Topping and filling:
- ½   **cup sugar**
- 1   **teaspoon cinnamon**
- 1   **cup chopped nuts**

Cream butter and gradually add sugar. Add eggs, one at a time. Sift together flour, baking powder and baking soda. Add to butter mixture and blend well. Add sour cream and vanilla extract and mix well.

In a separate bowl, mix together the sugar, cinnamon and nuts and set aside for filling and topping.

Spoon ½ of the cake batter into a sprayed 9 x 13 pan or tube pan. Cover with ½ of topping/filling mixture. Spoon other ½ of batter on top and then add rest of cinnamon-sugar topping.

Bake in a preheated 350 degree oven for 45 minutes. Test with a toothpick for doneness. Cool completely before cutting.

Freezes well.

APPLE CHEESE TORTE

Preheat oven to 350 degrees

Crust:
- 1   stick butter, room temperature
- 1/3   cup sugar
- 1/4   teaspoon vanilla extract
- 1   cup all purpose flour

Filling:
- 1   8 ounce package cream cheese, room temperature
- 1/4   cup sugar
- 1/2   teaspoon vanilla extract
- 1   egg

Topping:
- 4   cups apples, peeled and sliced (approximately 6 large apples)
- 1/3   cup sugar
- 1/2   teaspoon cinnamon
-     confectioners sugar

To make crust, cream butter and sugar. Add vanilla extract. Add flour and mix well. Pat dough into bottom of a 9 inch springform sprayed with non-stick cooking spray. Raise dough to about 2 inches on sides.

For topping: Toss sliced apples with sugar and cinnamon. Set aside.

In a large bowl combine filling ingredients until smooth. Pour filling into prepared crust. Top with apples and bake for 30 minutes in a preheated 350 degree oven. Cool for 1 hour. Unmold and dust with confectioners sugar.

PLAIN OLD BANANA CAKE

Preheat oven to 350 degrees

½	cup butter
1¼	cups sugar
2	eggs, lightly beaten
1	teaspoon baking soda
4	tablespoons sour cream
1	cup ripe bananas, mashed
1½	cups all purpose flour
1	teaspoon vanilla extract

In a mixer, cream butter and sugar. Add lightly beaten eggs and mix well. Stir in baking soda and sour cream. Beat well until blended. Add bananas, flour and vanilla extract. Mix well.

Pour batter into a 9 x 13 pan sprayed with non-stick cooking spray. Bake in a preheated 350 degree oven for one hour. Test with a toothpick.

When cool, cut into squares.

NUTTY CHOCOLATE CAKE

Preheat oven to 350 degrees

This cake freezes well and is very rich.

1½   **cups butter**
6   **eggs**
1½   **cups sugar**
2   **cups flour**
1   **package of powdered chocolate frosting mix**
2   **cups chopped walnuts**

Cream butter in large bowl at high speed. Add eggs one at a time, beating well after each addition. Gradually add sugar and continue beating until light and fluffy. By hand, stir in flour, frosting mix and walnuts until well blended.

Pour batter into a sprayed or greased bundt pan. Bake in a preheated 350 degree oven for 60-65 minutes. Cool 2 hours before removing from pan.

UNUSUAL SPICE CAKE

Preheat oven to 350 degrees

This cake is different because it has a meringue top.

Cake:
- 2⅔ cups cake flour
- 1 teaspoon baking soda
- 1 teaspoon baking powder
- 1 teaspoon ground cloves
- 1 teaspoon cinnamon
- ½ pound butter
- 2 cups brown sugar
- 2 eggs + 2 egg yolks
- 1 cup sour milk (to make sour milk add 1 tablespoon vinegar to milk)

Meringue:
- 2 egg whites
- 1 cup brown sugar
- ½ cup pecans or walnuts

Sift flour, baking soda, baking powder and spices 3 times. Cream butter and sugar until fluffy. Add eggs and yolks and beat thoroughly. Add sifted ingredients alternating with sour milk in small amounts. Pour into a greased 9 inch square pan.

Make meringue by whipping egg whites on high speed. Sprinkle brown sugar in while the machine is going until peaks form. Fold in nuts by hand. Spread meringue over the batter and bake in a preheated 350 degree oven for 1 hour.

SUNSHINE CAKE

Preheat oven to 325 degrees

You can bake this cake in a tube pan or in a 9 x 13. Either way, you'll love the delicious, delicate taste.

Cake:
Mix together:

7	eggs, separated
1	teaspoon cream of tartar
1⅓	cups sugar
4	tablespoons hot water or orange juice
1	cup cake flour
1	teaspooon vanilla extract
	small can of coconut

Frosting:
Beat together:

½	cup butter
2	cups confectioners sugar
2	tablespoons milk
1	teaspoon vanilla extract

———

Separate the eggs into two bowls. Beat egg whites with cream of tartar and ⅔ cup sugar until fluffy. Set aside.

Beat egg yolks with ⅔ cup sugar and add hot water or orange juice. Add cake flour, vanilla extract and a handful of coconut. Carefully, fold in the egg whites.

Pour batter into a sprayed tube or 9 x 13 pan. Bake for 1 hour in a preheated 325 degree oven.

Cool for 1 hour and frost. Sprinkle rest of coconut over top of cake.

Freezes well even with the frosting.

APPLE CINNAMON BUNDT CAKE

Preheat oven to 350 degrees

This cake is delicious right out of the oven or four days later!

Filling:
Mix together:
- ¼   cup sugar
- 3   large apples sliced and peeled
- ½   tablespoon cinnamon, set aside.

Cake Base:
Mix together:
- 2½   cups sugar
- 3   teaspoons baking powder
- ½   cup orange juice
- 2½   teaspoons vanilla extract
- 1   cup oil
- 4   eggs (lightly beaten)
- 3   cups unsifted flour
-    nuts (optional)

Frosting: (Optional)
Mix together:
- 1   cup confectioners sugar
- 1   teaspoon vanilla extract
- 3   tablespoons orange juice
- 1   teaspoon finely grated orange rind (optional)

In a greased bundt pan, pour in ½ cake base. Spread the apple mixture evenly over this layer. Then spread the other ½ of cake base mixture on top. Bake for 1½ - 1¾ hours in a preheated 350 degree oven. Test for doneness with toothpick.

Cool for 1 hour and then frost. The frosting will look more like a glaze.

Freezes well.

LEMON POUND CAKE

Cake:
- 1 **cup butter**
- 2 **cups sugar**
- 3 **eggs**
- 3¼ **cups cake flour**
- ½ **teaspoon baking soda**
- 1 **cup buttermilk**
- 2 **tablespoons grated lemon**
- 2 **tablespoons lemon juice or lemon extract**

Glaze:
- ⅓ **cup butter**
- 2 **cups confectioners sugar**
- 2-4 **tablespoons hot water**
- ½ **teaspoon lemon peel**

Cream butter and sugar until light and fluffy. Beat in eggs, one at a time. Add cake flour, baking soda and buttermilk to the mixture and stir until well blended. Stir in grated lemon and lemon juice.

Pour into a sprayed bundt pan and bake for 1 hour in a preheated 325 degree oven. When a toothpick comes out clean, the cake is done. Cool for at least one hour and then invert. Before glazing, make sure the cake is totally cooled.

To prepare glaze, mix butter and confectioners sugar. Add hot water and lemon peel. Mix well. Drizzle glaze over cake. Allow glaze to harden before serving or freezing.

BEST RUM CAKE EVER!!

This recipe comes from my friend Verna in Hawaii. She serves it for all her parties and it's really a "smash"! **This one's just for laughs!**

1 or 2 **quarts Rum**
    1   **cup butter**
    1   **teaspoon sugar**
    2   **large eggs**
    1   **cup dried fruit**
        baking powder
    1   **teaspoon soda**
        lemon juice
        brown sugar
        nuts

Before you start, sample the Rum to check for quality. Good isn't it? Now go ahead.

Select a large mixing bowl, measuring cup, etc. Check the Rum again. It must be just right. To be sure Rum is of the highest quality, pour one level cup of Rum into a glass and drink it as fast as you can. Repeat - with an electric mixer beat 1 cup of butter in a large fluffy bowl, add 1 seaspoon of thugar and beat again.

Meanwhile, make sure that the Rum is of the finest quality. Try another cup. Open second quart if necessary. Add 2 arge leggs, 2 cups fried druit and beat till high. If druit gets stuck in beaters, just pry it loose with a drewscriver.

Sample the Rum again, checking for tonscisticity. Next sift 3 cups of pepper or salt (it really doesn't matter). Sample the Rum again. Sift ½ pint of lemon juice. Fold in chopped butter and strained nuts. Add 1 babblespoon of brown thugar, or whatever color you find. Wix mel.

Grease oven and turn cake pan to 350 gredees. Not pur the whole mess into the coven, and ake. Check the Rum again, and go to bed.

NOTES

NOTES

JUST FOR STARTERS

Just For Starters

AVOCADO MOLD

1   **envelope unflavored Knox Gelatin**
¼   **cup cold water**
2   **packages frozen avocado dip, defrosted**
1   **mashed fresh avocado**
1   **6 ounce dry Italian seasoning dressing mix**
1   **pint sour cream**
2   **drops green food coloring**
½   **cucumber, peeled, seeded and chopped**
½   **can chopped black olives**
½   **pound cooked and cleaned baby shrimp**
2   **tablespoons caviar**

Spray a 9½ inch tart pan with non-stick cooking spray.

In a small sauce pan, sprinkle gelatin over cold water. Let sit for 5 minutes to soften. Cook over medium heat until mixture just comes to a boil and gelatin dissolves.

In a large bowl, mix the avocado dips and fresh avocado with Italian seasoning, sour cream and green food coloring. Add prepared gelatin and mix together. Pour mixture into sprayed pan and refrigerate until firm. **DO NOT FREEZE.**

Unmold and garnish with chopped cucumbers in a circular motion bordering the outermost edges of the pan. Follow with a border of black olives. Then, move in towards the center with circles of shrimp. Put caviar in the center of mold. Serve with crackers.

It looks beautiful and tastes great.

P.S. The green food coloring is used to maintain the "avocado" color instead of the brownish green color caused when avocados are exposed to the air.

ILENE'S SPINACH DIP

Ilene works market for us and she has made this dip for me for several years. We double this recipe.

- **10** **ounce package frozen chopped spinach, defrosted (squeeze out excess water)**
- **2** **cups mayonnaise (I use Hellmann's)**
- **5** **green onions, chopped**
- **⅓** **cup fresh chopped parsley**

Put all ingredients into a blender and mix well. Chill and enjoy.

This recipe looks great if you take a round bread and scoop out the middle and put spinach dip into center. Serve this with all your favorite vegetables for dipping.

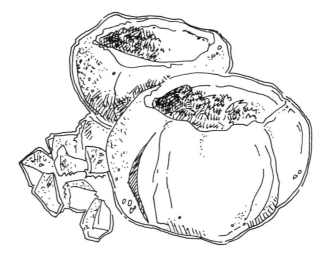

GAZPACHO MOLD

My friend Barbara gave me this recipe. I serve it with my Mexican lunch, but it's a great appetizer anytime!

2	envelopes unflavored gelatin
1/4	cup cold water
1/4	cup boiling water
2	cups mayonnaise (Hellmann's)
2	tomatoes, chopped and drained
1	green pepper, seeded and chopped
1	cucumber, peeled, seeded and chopped
1	small onion, chopped
1	cup celery, chopped
	salt and pepper

Dissolve gelatin with 1/4 cup cold water. Add 1/4 cup boiling water and stir to dissolve. Mix gelatin with mayonnaise. Add tomatoes, green pepper, cucumber, onion and celery. Blend well. Add salt and pepper to taste. Grease (or spray) small, 4 1/2 cup mold and pour in mixture. Chill at least 4 hours or overnight.

Run a knife carefully along sides of mold. Put a plate over the top and gently shake to unmold.

This recipe slices well and can be served as a side dish.

SHRIMP MOUSSE

This is a favorite at market time. My friend Barbara gave me this recipe. It can easily be doubled.

1	**envelope unflavored gelatin**
1/3	**cup cold water**
1	**cup tomato soup, not diluted**
1	**8 ounce cream cheese, softened**
1	**cup mayonnaise**
2	**4 1/2 ounce cans tiny shrimp, mashed**
1/2	**cup celery, chopped**
1/2	**cup onion, finely chopped**

Dissolve gelatin in 1/3 cup cold water. Set aside.

In a medium sized pot, bring soup to a boil. Add gelatin and stir well. Remove from heat.

Pour soup and gelatin mixture into a mixer and add softened cream cheese. Process until smooth. Stir in mayonnaise and add shrimp. Blend well. Add celery and onion and stir well.

Put mousse into a small 4 1/2 cup mold sprayed with non-stick cooking spray.

Refrigerate for at least 4 hours or overnight. Unmold and serve with crackers.

CAVIAR MOLD

Serves: 10-12

1	package unflavored gelatin
2	tablespoons lemon juice
2	tablespoons water
½	cup Hellmann's mayonnaise
½	cup Miracle Whip
2	tablespoons sour cream
	salt and pepper to taste
2	teaspoons Worcestershire sauce
1	4 ounce jar lumpfish caviar
½	small onion, grated
2	teaspoons anchovy paste
6	hard boiled eggs, chopped fine

Dissolve gelatin in small dish with lemon juice and water. Place in bowl of hot water until gelatin dissolves.

In another bowl, blend mayonnaise, Miracle Whip, sour cream, salt, pepper, Worcestershire sauce, caviar, onion and anchovy paste. Mix well by hand. Add chopped eggs and mix lightly but thoroughly. Stir in gelatin.

Use a 1½ pint ring mold that has been sprayed with non-stick cooking spray. Pour mixture into mold. Chill for 4 hours or more.

The mold can be made the day before.

Unmold and garnish with crackers or toast points.

This recipe can be doubled.

COLD CRABMEAT DIP

2 packages frozen crabmeat, defrosted
1 8 ounce cream cheese
1 3 ounce cream cheese
2 tablespoons mayonnaise (I use Hellmann's)
1 teaspoon Worcestershire sauce
Dash garlic powder
1 teaspoon lemon juice
1 whole chopped green onion
1 bottle Hoffman's Shrimp Cocktail Sauce
2 tablespoons chopped fresh parsley for garnishing
1-2 drops lemon juice (optional)
crackers for dipping

Defrost crabmeat and squeeze out any excess liquid. Set aside. In a mixer or Cuisinart with steel blade, blend cream cheese, mayonnaise, Worcestershire sauce, garlic powder, lemon juice and green onion. Process just until blended and creamy.

Put mixture into a round dish. Cover with cocktail sauce. Spread crabmeat on top and sprinkle enough parsley just to garnish. Sprinkle in a drop or two of lemon juice, if desired. Refrigerate at least 1 hour before serving. Serve with assorted crackers surrounding the dish. This is delicious and looks beautiful!

GAZPACHO

My friend Marlene made this soup for me at market time when I served my Mexican lunch. It was a great hit.

3 **19 ounce cans peeled whole tomatoes**
6 **cucumbers, peeled, seeded and chopped**
6 **green onions, chopped**
1 **green pepper, chopped**
2 **cloves garlic, chopped fine**
2 **stalks celery, chopped**
½ **cup olive oil**
½ **teaspoon dried dill weed**
1 **quart tomato juice**
½ **cup lemon juice, fresh squeezed (only)**
Tabasco to taste
dash of paprika

Optional:
2 **teaspoons Lawry's Seasoned Salt**
1 **tablespoon sugar**

Garnish:
chopped parsley
croutons
chopped hard boiled egg

Using a Cuisinart, fitted with a steel blade, individually chop tomatoes, cucumbers, green onions, green pepper, garlic and celery. Place each in separate bowl.

Combine olive oil and dill weed and process for 30 seconds. Add all the chopped vegetables and process with a few quick on/off pulses, just to blend.

Add tomato juice, lemon juice, Tabasco and paprika. If desired, add Lawry's seasoned salt and sugar. Process until well blended and the consistency you enjoy. Pour into a large pitcher and chill for at least 1 hour before serving.

Serve in small bowls or mugs. Have chosen garnishes available in individual bowls for your guests to top off their soup.

This is a hit as part of a Mexican dinner, on a hot summer day or anytime!

JOAN & GWEN'S SALMON MOUSSE

For the last 8 years Joan and Gwen have each made me this salmon mousse for every market. It's divine!

1	envelope unflavored gelatin
1/2	cup boiling water
2	tablespoons lemon juice
1	small onion, sliced
1/2	teaspoon salt
1/2	cup mayonnaise (I use Hellmann's)
1	16 ounce can red salmon, drained and boned
1	teaspoon dill weed
1/4	teaspoon paprika
1/2	cup heavy cream
	cucumber for garnish

Mix gelatin with boiling water. Combine with lemon juice and onion in a blender or Cuisinart fitted with steel blade. Process for 30 seconds. Add salt, mayonnaise, salmon, dill and paprika. Blend again, for 15 seconds. Add heavy cream and blend for an additional 15 seconds.

Pour into a sprayed 3 cup mold (fish mold is great). Cover with plastic wrap and refrigerate for at least 4 hours or overnight. Recipe may be made 2 days in advance. Unmold and decorate with sliced cucumbers.

Use the "Easy Cucumber Sauce" on the side if desired!

EASY CUCUMBER SAUCE

Cucumber sauce is great on the side of the Salmon Mousse or Salmon Loaf.

- **2 cups cucumbers, peeled, seeded and chopped**
- **1 cup sour cream**
- **1 tablespoon dill weed (I use fresh)**
- **1 tablespoon chopped chives**
- **½ teaspoon salt**

Combine all ingredients and chill.

★ ★ ★ ★ ★ ★ ★ ★ ★ ★ ★

NANCY AND DAVID'S RASPBERRY BAKED BRIE

★ ★ ★ ★ ★ ★ ★ ★ ★ ★ ★ ★ ★ ★ ★ ★ ★ ★ ★

Preheat oven to 350 degrees

Nancy and David design fabulous, innovative jewelry. Their contemporary silver pieces are worn with great pride. This brie recipe makes a terrific hors-d'oeuvre.

1	**package filo dough**
1	**mini brie**
1	**8 ounce jar raspberry preserves**
1	**3 ounce package almonds, sliced**
½	**stick butter, melted**

On a greased cookie sheet, spread several pieces of filo dough. Dough should be wide enough to completely cover brie.

Place brie in center of dough. Generously spread preserves on top of brie. Sprinkle sliced almonds over preserves.

Carefully lift filo dough to cover entire brie. If desired, crumble some additional filo dough on top to make crust flakier. Brush melted butter over entire crust.

Bake in a preheated 350 degree oven for 25 minutes. Remove from oven and let stand 10 minutes before serving.

SEAFOOD MOLD

Serves: 10-12

- 2 packages of Knox gelatin
- 2 cans of crabmeat, drained, reserving 3 tablespoons of liquid
- 1 can cream of mushroom soup, undiluted
- 1 8 ounce Philadelphia cream cheese, softened
- 1 can of shrimp, drained
- 3/4 cup celery, chopped
- 1 whole sweet onion, grated fine
- 3/4 cup Hellmann's mayonnaise
  celery chunks for garnish

Take 3 tablespoons of the liquid from canned crabmeat and stir into the gelatin. Add mushroom soup and bring to a boil.

Add softened cream cheese and stir until thoroughly dissolved.

Slowly blend in crabmeat, shrimp, celery, onion and mayonnaise and mix thoroughly by hand.

Pour into a small fish mold sprayed with non-stick cooking spray and refrigerate.

Unmold by running a knife carefully around mold. Place plate over mold, invert and shake gently to remove.

Garnish with celery chunks and crackers.

MY FAMOUS 7 LAYER AVOCADO PIE

Serves 40 people

I use a large round lucite platter that has a 1 inch lip all the way around. I've seen this done in throw-away foil pans. Thanks, Marsha!

5	**cans of Frito-Lay Bean Dip**
4	**cups sour cream**
1	**double package of taco seasoning (or 2 regular size)**
7	**cans frozen avocado dip, defrosted**
3	**cans sliced black olives**
5	**large tomatoes cut into small pieces and drained**
½	**cup chopped scallions (optional)**
1	**large package shredded cheddar cheese**
2	**bags nacho or taco chips for dipping**

Spread bean dip so it covers bottom of serving tray and just up the sides. Mix sour cream with taco seasoning and spread on top of bean dip to cover. Next, spread avocado dip over sour cream. Cover with olives, tomatoes, and scallions. Finally, a layer of cheddar cheese.

Refrigerate over night and enjoy with Nacho or Taco chips served on the side.

* For a smaller group, cut the recipe in half.

VERNA'S CHEESE BALL

2	8 ounce packages cream cheese, softened
1	10 ounce package - extra sharp Cheddar cheese, grated (Cracker Barrel)
1	tablespoon green pepper, chopped fine
1	tablespoon onion, minced
1-2	dashes Cayenne pepper (to taste)
1	teaspoon real lemon juice
1	teaspoon Worcestershire sauce
8	ounces walnuts, crushed

Mix together all ingredients except nuts and form 1 or 2 balls. Roll in crushed walnuts and chill. Can be frozen for later use.

SHRIMP PATÉ

1 3 ounce cream cheese (cut into cubes)
⅓ cup mayonnaise (I use Hellmann's)
3 tablespoons chopped onion
1 tablespoon white horseradish
1 teaspoon Dijon mustard
1 teaspoon dry dill
½ teaspoon sugar
½ teaspoon salt
1 tablespoon lemon juice
¼ teaspoon tabasco sauce
¾ pound cooked and cleaned small shrimp cut into small pieces
   (if canned, drain)

Crackers to garnish

In a food processor, fitted with a steel blade, or a blender, process cream cheese and mayonnaise, just until smooth. Add onion, horseradish, mustard, dill, sugar, salt, lemon juice and tabasco sauce and process until blended and smooth. Add shrimp and process until blended.

Remove mixture and shape into a ball. Wrap with wax paper and put in refrigerator for at least 4 hours or overnight. This can be prepared in advance and keeps for 3 days.

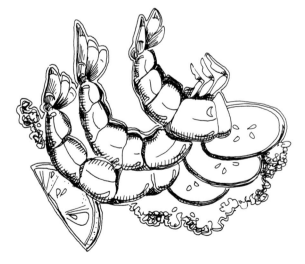

NOTES

NOTES

SIMPLY SALADS

Simply Salads

COOKIE'S SALAD TOSS-UP TIPS!

1. Eggs should be fresh, clean and unbroken. Bad eggs can be harmful because they contain certain bacteria. Eggs are best used within one week of purchase, but can last in the refrigerator up to five weeks.

2. Always refrigerate any recipes with eggs. Bacteria grows quickly.

3. Hard boiled eggs should be used within one week.

4. Never try to freeze a recipe that includes mayonnaise. The mayonnaise will separate! Once a jar of mayonnaise is opened, keep the remainder refrigerated.

5. Never marinate vegetables or meats in a metal container. Only use glass or plastic.

6. Anything which needs to be marinated for more than 1 hour should be refrigerated.

7. I always put a little non-stick cooking spray into the pot of boiling water, before adding the pasta. It cooks beautifully!

CHINESE CHICKEN SALAD

Serves 8 people

2   **pounds frozen chicken nuggets, breaded (found in freezer department or use leftover fried chicken cut into small pieces)**
2   **heads lettuce**
1   **can sliced water chestnuts, drained**
¼   **can bean sprouts**
¼   **pound pea pods cut in half**
1   **can or bag of chow mein noodles**
¼   **cup ketchup**
¼   **cup teriyaki sauce**
½   **cup honey**

Bake chicken as directed. Let cool. If chunks are large, cut into small pieces. In a large bowl, shred lettuce and add water chestnuts, sprouts, pea pods and noodles. Add chicken chunks and toss. Mix together ketchup, teriyaki sauce and honey in a small bowl. Pour just enough sauce over chicken salad to lightly cover, but not drench the salad. Toss lightly.

This recipe is a favorite. It's wonderful to serve with the Oriental Pasta and Orange Ambrosia Jello.

For a special treat — dip fortune cookies in melted white candy-making chocolate. Let dry on wax paper. Your company won't believe you did it.

ORIENTAL PASTA SALAD

I usually make 6 lbs. of this pasta recipe at a time! People can't get enough of it!
Especially my son, Jason.

1	pound pasta, any shape you want (even plain spaghetti works great)
1	8 ounce bottle teriyaki sauce
2	tablespoons soy sauce
2½	tablespoons sesame oil
1	can sliced water chestnuts
¼	pound fresh pea pods, broken in half
¼	cup fresh bean sprouts

Prepare the pasta according to the directions on the package. Rinse with cold
water and allow to come to room temperature.

Mix together teriyaki sauce, soy sauce, and sesame oil. Add water chestnuts, pea
pods and bean sprouts and stir together. Add prepared pasta and toss gently.

Refrigerate this recipe until cold. Then serve as a delicious side dish, lunch entree
or part of a buffet. It will stay in the refrigerator up to four days.

CHINESE BEANS

This is terrific to serve with my Chinese Chicken Salad!

2	pounds fresh raw string beans, broken in half
¾	cup teriyaki sauce (I use low-salt)
2	tablespoons sesame seeds
1	tablespoon sesame oil

Mix the teriyaki sauce, sesame seeds and oil in a bowl. Pour over beans and
marinate in the refrigerator overnight. The flavor is wonderful.

CHICKEN SALAD DIVINE

When we first started our business, I chose my mother's chicken salad recipe for my first luncheon. In fact, I have memories of my parents sitting in my kitchen taking apart chickens for hours. I still use this delicious recipe today . . . but I've gotten smart. Now I use just chicken breasts!

10	**skinless chicken breasts (with or without bones)**
3	**stalks of celery**
3/4-1	**cup Hellmann's mayonnaise**
1-3	**ounce bag sliced almonds**
20	**green or red seedless grapes, cut in half**
	Lawry's Seasoned Salt

Boil chicken breasts in a large pot of water until white and tender. (Approximately 20 minutes.) Drain chicken and let cool. (If you'd like, reserve the broth for a future chicken soup.) Cut into small chunks.

Chop celery into bite-size chunks and add to chicken. Stir in mayonnaise to coat. Add nuts and grapes and stir gently. Season with Lawry's Salt to taste. Mix gently.

Chill in refrigerator at least one hour before serving. Easy and delicious!

EGG SALAD SUPREME

Serves 6-8 people.

I make 18 dozen eggs into an egg salad mold every market. When I'm asked for the recipe, my buyers think I'm leaving out something because it seems too easy to be so delicious. The secret is to make sure you use a Cuisinart or blender for chopping eggs.

   1   **dozen eggs**
   5   **tablespoons Hellmann's mayonnaise**
   1   **teaspoon Lawry's Seasoned Salt**
       dash of pepper
       sour cream for garnish
       Lumpfish caviar for garnish

Boil eggs and peel. Place in a food processor fitted with steel blade. Using the on/off button chop eggs into small fine pieces. Do not overprocess. Add mayonnaise, Seasoned Salt and pepper. Stir just to combine.

Spray a 6-cup ring mold with non-stick cooking spray and pour in egg salad. Chill overnight. Unmold on a platter and put sour cream into the hole and cover top of the sour cream with lumpfish caviar.

Looks fabulous! Tastes great!

TUNA SALAD MOUSSE

I have stores that come in specifically for my tuna. It's so popular, I make 30 pounds at each market.

       2   **stalks of celery, chopped fine**
       2   **large cans water packed tuna**
       5   **rounded tablespoons Hellmann's mayonnaise**
     ½   **teaspoon Lawry's Seasoned Salt**
           dash of pepper

In a Cuisinart, fitted with a steel blade, chop stalks of celery. Squeeze excess water out of tuna and add to celery in Cuisinart and process with quick on/off pulses until almost smooth. Add mayonnaise and seasoning and stir by hand. Refrigerate at least 1 hour before serving.

Very easy - very good!

SANDWICH LOAF

Serves 12-14

I make these sandwich loaves at least twice a year. They look great on a platter. When my buyers slice into them, they think it's a layer cake.

Loaf
- **16 inch unsliced long loaf of bread (white, whole wheat, or mixed wheat are best.)**
- **Chicken Salad Divine**
- **Tuna Mousse**
- **Egg Salad Supreme**
- ***(Refer to individual recipes)***

Frosting
- **½ cup Hellmann's mayonnaise**
- **3 8 ounce packages of cream cheese**

Garnish (Optional)
- **2-3 chopped hard boiled eggs**
- **1 can sliced green olives**
- **1 can sliced black olives**
- **1 large cucumber, thinly sliced**

Remove the crust from a 16 inch long loaf of unsliced bread. (You can order that size from any bakery.) Turn loaf on side and cut into 4 even lengths. Spread each layer with a different salad. Use chicken salad, tuna salad, and egg salad. Ham salad is also very good as one of the layers.

Prepare frosting by combining the mayonnaise with cream cheese. Mix well by hand or put into Cuisinart fitted with a steel blade to get a smooth consistency. Spread over the whole loaf. Decorate with sliced hard boiled eggs, sliced olives, and/or sliced cucumbers.

Refrigerate for at least one hour before serving.

LEFTOVER LAYERED SALAD

    Tuna salad
    Egg salad
    Salmon salad
1-2   **cans frozen avocado spread, defrosted**
 ½   **teaspoon Good Season's Italian Dressing**
  8   **ounces sour cream**
    red or black caviar for garnish

Spray non-stick cooking spray in a springform pan large enough to hold your leftover salads. Layer salads one on top of the other, smoothing after each addition.

In a separate bowl, mix together ½ teaspoon of the Good Season's powdered dressing for each can of avocado spread that you use. The quantity will depend on the size of your pan.

Spread avocado mixture over salads. Refrigerate for 2 hours. Add a layer of sour cream and refrigerate for another few hours or overnight.

Before serving, put a dollop of caviar in the center or cover the entire top with caviar.

Unmold and serve with toast points and crackers.

Easy and delicious!

P.S. If you can't find the frozen avocado spread just blend a fresh avocado with a few drops of green food coloring. This keeps the color from turning brown. Then spread as directed.

TAFFY APPLE SALAD

I ate this at my sister-in-law's house and I had her write out this recipe immediately. I couldn't go home without it. Thanks Eda!

I make five times this recipe for my market. It takes 2 days to put it together but it's worth the time!

 1   **large can pineapple chunks in heavy syrup**
       Separate juice in one pot, chunks in another.
 2   **cups mini-marshmallows**
 1   **tablespoon flour**
1½ **tablespoons white-plain vinegar**
 1   **egg**
 ½ **cup sugar**
 1   **8 ounce Cool Whip**
1½ **cups Planter's Cocktail Peanuts**
 4   **peeled apples, red or green or a combination, cut in chunks**

---

1. Place pineapple chunks and marshmallows together in a pot and cover. Place in refrigerator overnight.

2. Cook pineapple juice, flour, vinegar, egg, and sugar over medium heat until thickens. Stir constantly. Refrigerate overnight. (Pick small pieces of white from egg out of cooked mixture.)

3. On second day, mix steps 1 and 2 together.

4. Add Cool Whip, nuts, and apples to mixture.

5. Refrigerate until serving. It really tastes like a taffy apple.

TACO SALAD

Serves 8

South of the border flavor in your own home.

2	heads lettuce
2	large tomatoes, chopped and drained
1½	pounds ground beef
1	package taco seasoning
½	large bottle Catalina Dressing
1	4 ounce package shredded cheddar cheese
¼	bag taco chips, crushed

Shred the lettuce in a bowl. Add chopped tomatoes. In a large fry pan, brown ground beef and drain off fat. Stir in taco seasoning. Add beef to lettuce and tomatoes and toss with Catalina dressing. Top with cheddar cheese and crushed taco chips.

If you want to serve the salad warm, put it out immediately. If you want the salad to be cold, prepare the beef and chill it in the refrigerator. Then assemble with the rest of the cold vegetables, dressing, cheese and chips before serving.

MEXICAN RICE SALAD

1　8 ounce box white rice
1　can garbanzo beans, drained
1　red pepper, chopped
1　green pepper, chopped
2　tablespoons scallions, chopped
1　8 ounce jar Catalina dressing

Cook rice according to package directions. Let cool and then toss in a large bowl with garbanzo beans, red pepper, green pepper, scallions and Catalina dressing.

Refrigerate until thoroughly chilled. Will stay fresh in the refrigerator for 3 days.

CORN SALAD WITH OLIVES

2　bags frozen niblets corn
1　green pepper, chopped
1　red pepper, chopped
1　can sliced black olives
1　8 ounce bottle Italian dressing

Mix all ingredients together and chill overnight. The flavor is delicious and makes a great side dish.

THE BEST CAESAR SALAD!

1   Romaine lettuce washed and chilled

Dressing:
1   can flat anchovies
2   cloves garlic
¼   cup olive oil
1   lemon
1   egg

Salt and pepper
1   cup freshly grated Parmesan cheese
croutons

Drain anchovies and put in bottom of a small bowl. Press cloves of garlic through press and mix with anchovies. Make into a paste by pressing with a fork into bottom and sides of bowl. Add olive oil a little at a time and continue mixing. Squeeze juice of a whole lemon with a fork into the mixture. Coddle the egg by boiling in water for 30 seconds. Add egg into the mixture and stir.

Break chilled lettuce into small pieces. Just before serving pour dressing over the lettuce. Add salt, pepper to taste and lightly sprinkle parmesan cheese. Add croutons and toss lightly!

Serve and enjoy!

ANTIPASTO PASTA SALAD

A very colorful presentation and delicious taste.

    1   **pound pasta, any shape**

Cut into bite-size pieces:
    1   **cup Mozzarella cheese**
    4   **slices of salami**
    ½   **cup red pepper**
    ½   **cup green pepper**
    ½   **cup yellow pepper**
        Can of baby corn
    1   **medium zucchini**

    1   **8 ounce jar of Kraft Italian Dressing**
        sprinkle with Parmesan cheese to taste

Mix all ingredients together. Chill thoroughly and serve.

EVERYDAY POTATO SALAD

Serves 10

5   pounds red potatoes, peeled, boiled and cooled
6   hard boiled eggs, cooked and sliced
2   stalks celery, cut into small chunks
1   cup small frozen peas
2   cups mayonnaise (I use Hellmann's)
2   teaspoons Lawry's Seasoned Salt

Peel potatoes and boil them in a large pot of water approximately 15 minutes. When a fork is easily inserted, yet potatoes are still firm, they are done. Allow them to cool and then cut into bite-size chunks or slices. Add eggs, celery and peas. Mix together mayonnaise and seasoning salt and add to potatoes. Mix well and refrigerate at least 1 hour before seasoning.

EASY AVOCADO PASTA

1   pound pasta, any size or shape
2   fresh avocados, peeled and cut into chunks
2   tomatoes, cut into chunks
1   bottle vinaigrette or Italian dressing (or use the Mustard Vinaigrette
     recipe in this book)

Cook pasta according to package directions. Drain and rinse with cold water. Put into large bowl and add avocado, tomatoes, and dressing. Toss gently and serve. Will stay fresh in refrigerator for 2 days.

TANGY COLD VEGETABLE PASTA SALAD

Serves 10-12

2	cups broccoli
2	cups cauliflower
2	cups carrots
2	cups celery
2	cups zucchini
2	cups pea pods
1	cup red pepper
1	cup green pepper
1	large bottle Kraft Italian Salad Dressing
1½	pounds pasta, spirals
1	bottle chili sauce
2	tablespoons lemon juice
6	tablespoons Dippity-Dill mix

Cut up all vegetables into bite-size pieces. In a large bowl, marinate vegetables in Italian dressing overnight.

The next day, prepare pasta according to the package instructions. Drain and rinse with cold water. Drain marinade from vegetables, reserving ½ cup of dressing, and toss lightly with pasta.

Combine chili sauce, lemon juice and Dippity-Dill in a small bowl. Pour over pasta and vegetables and toss to coat. Add remainder of Italian marinade to taste.

Refrigerate until thoroughly chilled and serve!

CAESAR SALAD PASTA

1   pound pasta, any small shape
1   8 ounce bottle Caesar dressing - or see The Best Caesar Salad Dressing
        recipe
1   Romaine lettuce, rinsed well and chopped into chunks
1   box croutons
     grated Parmesan cheese: to taste

Cook pasta according to directions. Drain and rinse with cold water. Add dressing, lettuce, croutons, and cheese. Toss and serve. This is a wonderful addition to any meal or serve by itself.

QUICK SEAFOOD PASTA

1   pound pasta, shell shaped
1   pound small cooked and cleaned shrimp or crab meat, cut into chunks
        (or use the artificial seafood sticks)
¼   pound little frozen peas, defrosted
3   celery stalks, cut into chunks
1   cup mayonnaise (Hellmann's)
3   tablespoons ketchup
     (Instead of mayonnaise and ketchup, an 8 ounce bottle of Russian
        Dressing may be used.)

Cook pasta according to package directions, drain and rinse with cold water. Put pasta in a large bowl. Add chunked seafood, peas and celery and stir. Combine mayonnaise and ketchup. Pour dressing over pasta and chill for 4 hours or overnight.

TORTELLINI PASTA ITALIANO

1½ pounds tri-color tortellini pasta (or any tortellini)
1 bottle Seven Seas Viva Herbs & Spices Dressing
1 package frozen small Le Sur Peas
1 can sliced water chestnuts
1 red pepper, chopped in small pieces
¼ pound salami, cut into strips

Prepare tortellini according to package instructions. Drain and rinse well. Add remaining ingredients to the pasta and stir to coat.

Refrigerate for at least 4 hours before serving.

This is quick, easy and delicious!

SWEET COLD NOODLES

This is a great cold pasta. I made this one up when I was in the mood for something solid as well as something sweet.

1 pound broad egg noodles
1 pound cottage cheese
1 cup sugar
2 tablespoons cinnamon
1 cup raisins

Cook pasta according to package direction. Drain and rinse with cold water. Pour into large bowl and mix in cottage cheese, sugar, cinnamon, and raisins. Chill overnight and enjoy.

SNAPPY POTATO SALAD

This potato salad looks very festive and tastes superb! I make 40 pounds of this potato salad at a time.

>   5   **pound bag red potatoes**
>   1   **bottle Seven Seas Viva Herbs and Spices Dressing**
>   1   **3 ounce jar capers, drained**
>   **fresh parsley, chopped (approximately ½ cup)**
>   1   **whole cabbage for garnish — red or purple**

Boil potatoes in a large pot of water for approximately 45 minutes until a fork is easily inserted into potatoes and yet they are still firm. Do not remove potato skins. When cool, cut into bite-size pieces and place in a large bowl. Add dressing, capers and just enough chopped parsley for color. Stir well to coat.

Line a bowl with the cabbage leaves for color and fill with potato salad.

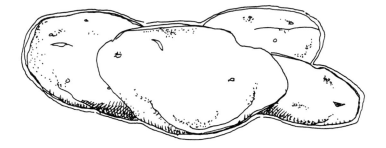

MUSTARD VINAIGRETTE

 1 **clove garlic, minced**
    or
 1 **clove shallots**
 ¾ **cup Safflower oil**
 ¼ **cup vinegar**
 ½ **teaspoon salt**
 ½ **teaspoon sugar (or sugar substitute)**
 3 **tablespoons water**
 2 **tablespoons Dijon mustard**

In a blender or food processor equipped with a steel blade, mince garlic or shallot. Add oil, vinegar, salt, sugar, water and Dijon mustard and process until well blended.

This dressing is delicious poured over salads or used as a marinade for chicken.

Refrigerate after preparing and shake well before serving.

LORENZO DRESSING

 1 **bunch watercress**
 4 **ounces chili sauce**
    Tabasco sauce — to taste
 1 **teaspoon Worcestershire sauce**
 2 **cups salad oil**
 ½ **cup apple cider vinegar**
 1 **teaspoon salt (or to taste)**
 ⅛ **teaspoon white pepper (or to taste)**

Using a food processor fitted with a steel blade, or a blender, chop up watercress and then add rest of ingredients. Blend until smooth.

Chill well before using!

FANCY STEAK SALAD

My buyers think I'm serving the most extravagant lunch when I serve this salad!!

1	**green pepper**
3	**cups broccoli**
3	**cups fresh pea pods**
3	**pounds flank steak, cut into strips**
6	**tablespoons peanut oil**
1	**8 ounce bottle teriyaki sauce**
2½	**tablespoons sesame oil**
1	**small can water chestnuts, sliced and drained**

Wash, dry and cut the green pepper, broccoli and pea pods into bite-size pieces. Set aside.

Sauté the steak in peanut oil until meat is tender and browned. Drain excess fat. Add teriyaki sauce, sesame oil and stir to coat meat.

Pour meat into large bowl with vegetables and add water chestnuts. Toss to mix and refrigerate for 4 hours or overnight.

Salad should be served very cold!

MOROCCAN COUSCOUS SALAD

You don't have to be Moroccan to enjoy this salad.

Serves 12 people

- 1   **10 ounce box couscous (Moroccan Pasta)**
- 1   **16 ounce bottle Italian dressing**
- 1   **cup bite-size pieces green pepper**
- 1   **cup bite-size pieces red pepper**
- 1   **cup bite-size pieces chick peas**
- 1   **cup bite-size pieces mushrooms**

Cook couscous according to package directions. Stir in Italian dressing. Add vegetables and mix well. Refrigerate overnight.

NOTES

ALWAYS ROOM FOR JELLO

Always Room For Jello

THINGS TO KNOW ABOUT JELLO!

It's probably been a long time since you've thought of serving jello as a side dish or dessert. You'll be surprised at the delightful reaction you'll receive when serving my jello molds. They are delicious, refreshing and beautiful to serve.

Here are a few "tips" to help make your jello turn out just right!

1. Spray your molds well with non-stick cooking spray. This will help them to come out easily.

2. Any recipe that calls for "sour cream" can use Cool Whip as a substitute in equal amounts. Any recipe made with Cool Whip can remain in the refrigerator up to 1 week.

3. Be sure the jello does not get hard before you are to add other ingredients. It should only be just starting to thicken.

4. To help quicken the "thickening" process, I often place the bowl in the freezer for a few minutes. Watch it because it starts to gel quickly. Also, you never want ice particles to form.

5. To create a "marbleized jello" choose a few favorite flavors. Chill until slightly thickened and whip with 1 cup of Cool Whip for a 6 ounce size jello. Pour the flavors into a greased bundt pan in layers. Then take a knife and swirl it through the layers in an "S" pattern. Chill for at least 4 hours, then unmold and serve.

CHOCOLATE BOTTOM RASPBERRY FLUFF

This creates a beautiful presentation and has a delicate, delicious taste!

Bottom:
- 1 **package chocolate wafers, crushed**
- ½ **cup sugar**
- ⅓ **cup melted butter**

- 1 **large package raspberry Jello**
- 2 **cups boiling water**
- 1 **cup orange juice**
- ½ **cup sugar**
- 1 **large can Pet Evaporated Milk, chilled**
- ½ **box frozen raspberries (defrost and drain juice well)**

Mix together chocolate wafers, sugar and melted butter and pat ¾'s of mixture into springform pan sprayed with non-stick cooking spray.

Blend Jello with boiling water and add orange juice and sugar. Chill for ½ hour. In a mixer, beat evaporated milk into peaks. Add chilled Jello and raspberries. Beat until raspberry color comes through.

Pour into crust and sprinkle with remaining ½ of cookie crumbs. Chill thoroughly, at least 4 hours or overnight. Remove sides of springform and serve.

HAWAIIAN DELIGHT

2 packages cherry Jello
2 packages lemon Jello
4 cups hot water
2 pints vanilla ice cream
2 cups sour cream
1 can sliced pineapple rings, drained
1 jar maraschino cherries

Place cherry Jello in one bowl and lemon Jello in another. Add 2 cups hot water to each and stir to dissolve. Chill until slightly thickened.

Whip each Jello separately. To each, add 1 pint of ice cream and 1 cup of sour cream. Beat well.

Place lemon Jello in sprayed bundt pan first. Put pineapple slices on top of whipped lemon Jello. Place a cherry in the center of each pineapple slice.

Pour whipped cherry Jello over pineapple slices and gently smooth to fill pan.

Refrigerate at least 4 hours or overnight.

Unmold and garnish with remaining fruit.

LEMON MOUSSE JELLO

This simple recipe is one of my favorites! People ask for it all the time.

1   **6 ounce package lemon Jello**
2   **cups boiling water**
2   **cups cold water**
1   **small carton lemon yogurt**
1   **12 ounce Cool Whip**
    fresh strawberries, for garnish

Make lemon Jello as directed and chill until not quite firm. Add lemon yogurt and whip in the Cool Whip. Pour into a bundt pan sprayed with non-stick cooking spray or spoon into a bowl and refrigerate for 3 hours or overnight.

Unmold by running a knife gently around the edges and turn over on a platter. Shake gently to remove from pan. Garnish with fresh strawberries.

FINGER JELLO

Yield: 100

This recipe comes from my friend Toddy. These are fun to take on a picnic!

4   **envelopes Knox unflavored gelatin**
3   **boxes flavored Jello (3 ounce size), any flavor**
3   **cups boiling water**

In a large bowl combine Knox unflavored gelatin and 3 flavored Jellos. Add boiling water and stir until dissolved. Pour into a large cookie sheet, with sides, that has been sprayed with non-stick cooking spray. Chill until firm.

Cut Jello into small squares. These can be picked up by hand and eaten like candy. Children love them. Adults can't stop eating them.

ORANGE AMBROSIA JELLO MOLD

1	6 ounce orange Jello
2	cups boiling water
1	pint frozen orange sherbet
2	small cans mandarin oranges, drained
2	small cans pineapple chunks, drained
½	cup mini marshmallows
½	cup flaked coconut
1	cup sour cream

In a large bowl, dissolve Jello with 2 cups boiling water. Add frozen sherbet and mix until dissolved. Add mandarin oranges and pineapple chunks and refrigerate until thickened, but not set. Mix marshmallows, coconut and sour cream and combine with Jello. Chill again until firm. Pour into a sprayed or greased 6 cup Jello mold (or into a large glass bowl) and chill 9 hours or overnight.

You can do basically the same recipe using raspberry sherbet and raspberries instead of mandarin oranges.

I triple this recipe for a large crowd and put it into an institutional size, 24 cup mold.

RASPBERRY MOUSSE JELLO

1	6 ounce raspberry Jello
2	cups boiling water
2	cups cold water
1	8 ounce carton raspberry yogurt
½	bag frozen raspberries, without juice (Wilderness brand if possible), defrosted
	or
1	cup fresh raspberries
1	12 ounce Cool Whip

Dissolve Jello and chill until almost firm. Add yogurt, raspberries, and Cool Whip and whip together. Pour into a bundt pan sprayed with non-stick cooking spray, or spoon into individual glasses or bowls.

Chill for at least 4 hours or overnight.

Options:
> **peach Jello and peaches**
> **cherry Jello and cherries**
> **strawberry/banana Jello and fruit**
> ***Make sure to use the same flavor for both the yogurt and Jello.**

To make chocolate filigree garnish, as shown on cover:

> **3 ounces chocolate**
> **few drops vegetable oil**
> **parchment paper**

Melt chocolate over double boiler. Smear back of cookie sheet with vegetable oil and smooth a sheet of parchment paper onto it.

Scrape chocolate into plastic bag. Cut tiny hole at corner. Pipe out filigree designs. Increase size of hole to achieve desired effect.

Set chocolate in cool place to harden. Do not refreigerate. Gently peel off parchment to free pieces.

ORANGE PINEAPPLE MOLD

1   6 ounce frozen orange juice
    undiluted, defrosted
2   3 ounce packages orange gelatin
1   pint sour cream
4   tablespoons marshmallow cream fluff
1   large can crushed pineapple with juice

In a medium saucepan, bring orange juice, orange gelatin, sour cream and marshmallow cream to a boil. Stir constantly until all ingredients are dissolved and smooth.

Remove from heat. Add can of crushed pineapple with juice and stir until blended.

Pour into sprayed 6½ cup mold and chill in refrigerator at least 4 hours or overnight.

NOTES

SOME LIKE IT HOT!

Some Like It Hot!

OSCAR DE LA RENTA'S LEMON CHICKEN

★ ★ ★ ★ ★ ★ ★ ★ ★ ★ ★ ★ ★ ★ ★ ★ ★ ★ ★

Serves 4

Oscar de la Renta is certainly one of the elite of the American fashion design community. His glamorous, elegant creations make every woman who wears them feel like a star. This is a quick and easy recipe for a wonderfully light and tasty dish!

4	**boneless, skinless breasts of chicken**
1	**cup chicken broth**
¼	**cup olive oil**
2½	**cups fresh lemon juice**
1	**tablespoon scallions**
3	**tablespoons cilantro**
1	**tablespoon white wine vinegar**

Cut each chicken breast into four long pieces. Place chicken and broth in frying pan and cook on medium heat for ten minutes. Remove chicken and place in serving dish.

To broth, add olive oil, lemon juice and scallions and bring to a boil. Simmer for one minute and pour over chicken.

Sprinkle cilantro and white wine vinegar over dish to taste.

BING CHERRY DUCK

Preheat oven to 325 degrees

A dish that's guaranteed to be all it's "quacked" up to be.

1   rack for roasting

1   duck, quartered
    Lawry's Seasoned Salt
    paprika
1   can dark pitted cherries in sauce
1   tablespoon cornstarch

Spray roasting pan and rack well with non-stick cooking spray.

Place quartered duck on rack. Place rack in roasting pan and season with Lawry's and paprika. Roast duck for at least 4 hours in a preheated 325 degree oven until all the grease is on pan bottom and duck is dry and crispy.

In a heavy pot, heat can of cherries. Add corn starch and stir until sauce thickens. Pour sauce over quartered duck and serve with brown rice or wild rice.

A favorite green vegetable completes this beautiful plate.

BILL BLASS' MEAT LOAF

★ ★ ★ ★ ★ ★ ★ ★ ★ ★ ★ ★ ★ ★ ★ ★ ★ ★ ★ ★

Serves 6   *Preheat oven to 350 degrees*

Bill Blass is one of 7th Avenue's most respected designers and one of the major forces in the fashion industry. However, when asked for his recipe he replied, "I may not go down in history for my clothes — but the meat loaf will be my claim to immortality!"

1	cup celery, chopped
1	cup onions, chopped
2	tablespoons butter
2	pounds chopped sirloin
1/2	pound veal, ground
1/2	pound pork, ground
1/2	cup parsley
1/3	cup sour cream
1 1/2	cups bread crumbs (soft)
1	egg, beaten
1	tablespoon Worcestershire sauce
	Pinch Thyme and Marjoram
	Salt and pepper to taste
1	bottle Heinz chili sauce
3	strips bacon

Saute celery and onions in butter. Combine sirloin, veal and pork. Add remaining ingredients and form loaf. Top with chili sauce and bacon strips.

Bake in preheated 350 degree oven for one hour.

Serve with crisp baked potato skins.

DIET CHICKEN DELIGHT

Serves 6   *Preheat oven to 350 degrees*

Whenever my husband Barry decides to go on a diet, he requests this low-cal dinner. It's great for company dinners and luncheons too!

- **4** **chicken breasts split, boned and skinned**
- **1** **8 ounce bottle of low-cal Italian Dressing**
     dash of low salt, seasoning salt
- **2** **Idaho potatoes, peeled and cut into pieces lengthwise**
     sprinkle of Parmesan cheese (optional)
- **1** **package of frozen Le Sur Peas, defrosted**

In a 9 x 13 ovenproof glass pan, marinate the chicken in Diet Italian Dressing overnight. The next day, sprinkle the chicken with low-cal seasoning salt. Add potatoes and turn to coat well with dressing.

Bake in a preheated 350 degree oven for 30 minutes. Turn chicken and continue cooking an additional 30 minutes.

Sprinkle lightly with Parmesan cheese, then defrosted peas. Place under the broiler until chicken is crisp. Watch to prevent burning!

Delicious! A complete meal in one pan.

★ ★

ADRIENNE LANDAU'S HUNGARIAN GOULASH

★ ★ ★ ★ ★ ★ ★ ★ ★ ★ ★ ★ ★ ★ ★ ★ ★ ★ ★ ★

Serves 4

Adrienne Landau is the rising star of the fur industry. Adrienne says "This dish always brings out the gypsy in me. Everytime I have this dish, it takes me back to my childhood when my grandfather and mother used to make it. Then we'd top it off with a dessert of chocolate eclairs!"

2	**tablespoons chicken fat**
4	**onions, chopped**
½	**green pepper, chopped**
	dash of salt
3	**cloves garlic**
2	**tablespoons Hungarian paprika**
2	**pounds beef cubes, trimmed**
½	**cup water**
1	**chicken bouillon cube**
1	**bag fresh sauerkraut**
1-2	**cups sour cream**

Grease bottom of a stew pot with chicken fat. Saute chopped onions until clear. Add green pepper and salt. Add garlic and enough paprika to make the color a true red.

Add beef cubes and water. Keep stirring to blend. Add chicken cube, stir to dissolve and simmer for 15 minutes. Continue to add small amounts of water at intervals while simmering.

Rinse sauerkraut with cold water and add to beef mixture. Allow to simmer for 1½ to 2 hours until tender. Stir occasionally. Add a little more water if needed for gravy consistency.

Before serving, mix sour cream to taste! This is delicious served with boiled potatoes or on a bed of broad egg noodles.

MICROWAVE FISH

I always use Lake Superior white fish.

> **2** **pounds Lake Superior white fish, boned and cut in half**
> **Lawry's Seasoned Salt to taste**
> **Pepper to taste**
> **¼** **cup milk**
> **½** **bottle chili sauce**
> **1** **orange, sliced**

Spray a microwave baking pan with non-stick cooking spray. Place fish in pan with skin side down. Season with pepper and Lawry's Seasoned Salt. Mix milk with chili sauce and pour over fish. Place sliced orange around the fish. (The milk will cut the fish smell in your kitchen.) Cook on high for 8½ minutes and serve immediately.

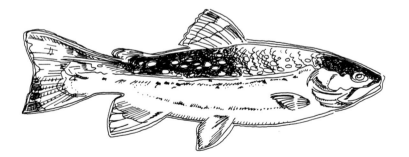

MICROWAVE MEAT LOAF

Serves 4-6

2 **pounds chopped meat**
1 **egg**
2 **tablespoons seasoned bread crumbs**
Lawry's salt to taste
pepper to taste
garlic powder to taste
2 **tablespoons milk**
½ **bottle chili sauce**
2 **rounded tablespoons brown sugar**

Spray microwaveable loaf pans with non-stick cooking spray.

Mix chopped meat with egg, bread crumbs and seasonings and milk.

Form meat into a rectangular shape and place into loaf pan. Cover top with chili sauce and brown sugar. Cover with wax paper and cook on high for 10 minutes.

GRANDMA FRAN'S MEAT, PRUNES AND POTATOES

This is an old Russian family recipe. My mother-in-law makes this for every holiday and calls it "Flaumen and Potatoes". It's always a favorite . . . especially with the men.

5	pounds chuck roast
5	pounds potatoes
1	box prunes
½	cup brown sugar
½	bottle chili sauce
1	large onion, sliced
½	8 ounce jar grape jelly
2	bunches carrots, cut into large pieces

Put all ingredients in a large pot. Cover and simmer for about 3 hours on top of stove on low heat.

Spray a large oven pan with non-stick cooking spray and pour in the entire stew. Place in a 300 degree oven for another 3 hours or until meat is very tender - falling off the fork.

You have a complete meal in one dish!

★ ★
JUDITH LEIBER'S TRANSYLVANIAN GULYA'S

★ ★ ★ ★ ★ ★ ★ ★ ★ ★ ★ ★ ★ ★ ★ ★ ★ ★ ★

Designer Judith Leiber is famous for her fabulous purses and belts. Her jeweled style is renown in the world of fashion. This recipe is a real "gem" too!

4	pounds sauerkraut
1/4	pound margarine
4	large white onions, minced
2	tablespoons tomato paste
2	bouillon cubes
	paprika to taste
1 1/2	pounds pork cut into 3/4" cubes and salted
2	sticks Hungarian cooking sausage or Polish Kilbasza or Kosher frankfurters
1	large container sour cream
1/2	pound mushrooms
2	green peppers

Wash sauerkraut, drain in colander. Put in large pot without water. Cook on slow heat for 1 1/2 hours, checking occasionally and adding a little water only if needed.

Melt margarine in large pan. Add minced onions and simmer tightly covered until wilted, for about 20 minutes. Add paprika, tomato paste and bouillon cubes. Add cut up pork. When done, mix with sauerkraut adding the rounds of sausage and 1/2 of the sour cream, mushrooms and 1 green pepper, chopped. Cook 1 hour longer.

This dish is better cooled, refrigerated and warmed up the next day. When ready to serve, mix the other half of the sour cream and garnish with rounds of green pepper.

ISAAC MIZRAHI'S "YEBRA" AND PRUNE BUTTER SAUCE

★ ★ ★ ★ ★ ★ ★ ★ ★ ★ ★ ★ ★ ★ ★ ★ ★ ★

Middle Eastern Stuffed Grape Leaves with Dried Apricots

Isaac Mizrahi is a hot, young contemporary designer. His innovative fashions are catching the eye of the American fashion scene.

This recipe is an example of the complicated dishes he likes to prepare and loves to eat. It was one of his grandmother's specialties. When he was a boy he used to peel off the grape leaves and just eat the filling, which annoyed her immensely. Since he's grown up he's acquired a passionate taste for the complete dish which he and his mother often make.

1	small jar grape leaves
2/3	cup white rice, short grain
1	tablespoon vegetable oil
1	teaspoon cinnamon
1	teaspoon allspice
1	teaspoon salt
1	pound ground beef or veal
1/2	cup water
15	dried apricot halves

Carefully remove grape leaves from jar and rinse in bowl of cold water. Wash rice and in large bowl combine with vegetable, oil, cinnamon, allspice and salt. Add ground beef and water. Mix thoroughly with hands. Mixture should be soft.

Taking one grape leaf at a time, remove stem (if any) with sharp knife. At base of leaf, place meat/rice mixture horizontally in long mound, not quite to edges of leaf, and roll carefully and tightly, folding in side to completely enclose mixture. Finished yebra should look like a cigar.

Place finished "cigars" in roaster and cover with prune butter sauce (recipe below), topping with apricot halves. Put aluminum foil directly on top of grape leaves and weigh down with a glass or oven proof plate.

Cook on stove top for 10 minutes, medium flame. Cover with lid and bake in preheated 350 degree oven for at least 2 hours. Add a little more water if all liquid evaporates when baking.

Prune Butter Sauce:
- **1 jar prune butter**
- **lemon juice**
- **⅓ cup sugar**
- **2 cups water**

In a sauce pan add prune butter. Refill same jar with lemon juice and stir in, along with ⅓ cup sugar. Cook over medium flame for 10 - 15 minutes.

Using ½ of sauce, dilute with 2 cups water. Pour over stuffed grape leaves. (Remaining sauce may be stored in refrigerator for several months.)

★ ★ ★ ☆ ☆ ★ ☆ ★ ★ ☆ ★ ☆ ☆ ☆ ☆ ☆ ☆ ☆ ★

ALBERT AND PEARL NIPON'S BRISKET WITH KASHA AND BOW TIES

★ ★ ★ ★ ★ ★ ★ ★ ★ ★ ★ ★ ★ ★ ★ ★ ★ ★ ★

Serves 6   *Preheat oven to 450 degrees*

Albert and Pearl Nipon have been a top name in dress designing for many years. These recipes were originally from Pearl's grandmother. They have always been family favorites, served as a complete meal with applesauce and coleslaw.

Brisket:
- 3 **pounds brisket, first cut**
- **salt and pepper**
- **garlic powder**
- **Lawry's Seasoned Salt**
- 1 **package Goodman's Onion Soup**

Kasha:
- 1 **package whole grain groats**
- 1 **egg**
- **salt and pepper**
- 2 **cups hot water**
- **pasta bow ties**

Season meat well with salt, pepper, garlic powder and Lawry's Seasoned Salt. Roast in preheated 450 degree oven for 15 minutes. Turn over and continue browning for an additional 15 minutes.

Dilute onion soup with amount of water called for on package. (More water might be added if more gravy is desired.) Add it to roasting pan and cover with heavy duty tin foil. Reduce oven temperature to 425 degrees and continue cooking for an additional 2 hours or until fork comes out of meat easily.

To prepare groats: mix whole grain groats with egg, salt and pepper in shallow pan. Cook over low heat until dry. Add hot water, cover and allow to simmer on low flame until water is absorbed and groats are tender (check package).

Boil bow ties as directed on package. Drain and mix with cooked groats. Add a little gravy from brisket.

Slice brisket thin and serve with groats and bow tie mixture (Kasha) as a wonderful side dish.

SHRIMP CREOLE

Serves 4-6

Every time I had to impress and entertain at the same time, this recipe was always a winner.

- 3 tablespoons vegetable oil
- ½ cup chopped onions
- ½ cup chopped celery
- 1 clove garlic, minced
- 2 cups canned tomatoes
- 1 8 ounce can tomato sauce
- 1½ teaspoons salt
- 1 teaspoon sugar
- ½ teaspoon chili powder (optional ½ teaspoon more if you like it a little hotter)
- 1 tablespoon Worcestershire sauce
- ¼ teaspoon tabasco sauce
- 1 teaspoon cornstarch
- 2 teaspoons water
- 1 pound raw, cleaned shrimps
- ½ cup chopped green pepper

In a large pan cook onion, celery, and garlic in hot oil until tender but not brown. Add tomatoes, tomato sauce, salt, sugar, chili powder, Worcestershire sauce and tabasco. Cook over low heat for 35 minutes uncovered

Mix cornstarch with water and stir into the sauce mixture. Cook until sauce thickens.

Add shrimp and green pepper. Cover and cook for about 5 minutes until shrimp is cooked through, but green pepper is still crunchy.

I serve this around a rice ring that is filled with Le Sueur peas.

★ ★ ★ ★ ★ ★ ★ ★ ★ ★ ★ ★ ★ ★ ★ ★

MARIA RODRIGUEZ' HUICHINANGO ALA PUERTO VALLARTA

★ ★ ★ ★ ★ ★ ★ ★ ★ ★ ★ ★ ★ ★ ★ ★ ★ ★ ★

(Puerto Vallarta Style Red Snapper)

Maria Rodriguez is bringing stardom to the Chicago fashion industry. Not only does she weave magic into her unique fabrics, but her designs have placed her in a class by herself. Maria got this recipe from friends who own the "Marisol - No. 11" Restaurant in the old market place in Puerto Vallarta. This dish is a favorite of Maria's, and her husband, Brad Cole.

Seasoned Dressing (to be prepared three days in advance)

⅔	**cup garlic, minced**
⅓	**cup parsley, minced**
4	**bay leaves, crushed**
1	**teaspoon black pepper**
	vinegar
	pure virgin olive oil

Place all spices in a one litre jar and fill 60% with vinegar and 40% olive oil. Let stand three days.

(This dressing may be stored and used all summer long when you grill shrimp, orange roughy, or similar whole fish.)

Preparation:

4 whole fresh red snappers (approximately 1-2 pounds each)

Diagonally slit fish in 5 areas. Sea salt and flour the entire fish. Grill on one side, turn over and spoon ample amount of the above dressing on fish. Repeat on reverse side. Regrill first side and add more dressing.

(Note: for red snapper, allow a total of 10 minutes of grilling time per 1 inch of thickness.)

When properly grilled, the bones of red snapper should easily separate from fish.

Serve with spanish rice mixed with peas and chopped carrots, refried pinto beans, a side of lettuce, tomatoes, black olives and warmed fresh corn tortillas.

THE BEST QUICHE LORRAINE

Preheat oven to 375 degrees

1	frozen pie crust, defrosted
1	stick butter
1	cup onions, chopped
1	cup mushrooms, chopped (fresh or canned)
1/2	cup Swiss cheese, grated
1	tablespoon flour
3	eggs
3/4	cup half and half cream
1	teaspoon salt
1/8	teaspoon pepper

In a large skillet, melt butter and sauté onions and mushrooms. Onions should be translucent. Place onions and mushrooms on bottom of pie crust.

Mix grated Swiss cheese with flour. Sprinkle cheese mixture over onions and mushrooms.

Beat eggs with half and half. Add salt and pepper and stir well. Pour over cheese.

Bake in a preheated 375 degree oven for 40 minutes.

Cool slightly before slicing and serving.

Optional additions (substituted for onions and mushrooms):
    green pepper
    tomatoes
    asparagus
    broccoli
    ham*
    salami*
These ingredients do not have to be sautéed.

★ ★ ★ ★ ★ ★ ★ ★ ★ ★ ★ ★ ★ ★ ★ ★ ★

DONNA KARAN'S CRISPY DIJON CHICKEN

★ ★ ★ ★ ★ ★ ★ ★ ★ ★ ★ ★ ★ ★ ★ ★ ★ ★

Donna Karan creates the most outstanding sportswear for the "woman on the go
. . . who has a very busy life style!" Her sophisticated sportswear appears under
her own label and also the new, and exciting DKNY. This recipe is one of Donna's
favorites! She suggests serving it hot with an asparagus salad, or it's great to serve
for a picnic with a big salad and lots of whole grained Italian bread, grilled with
herbs and pureed olive spread.

1	free-range chicken, cut into 8 pieces
	garlic flavored oil
	fresh ground pepper
½	cup white wine
⅓	cup Dijon mustard
1	cup crushed whole grain cereal flakes

Place chicken pieces in broiling or roasting pan with low sides. Brush pieces lightly
with garlic oil. Sprinkle with fresh ground pepper to taste.

Broil chicken, skin side down until opaque and beginning to brown. Turn chicken
over and repeat.

Mix wine and mustard to make marinade. Brush mixture on chicken and sprinkle
generously with cereal flakes. Broil chicken again until crispy and brown. Repeat
on other side.

Turn oven to bake and reduce temperature to 350 degrees. Continue to cook
chicken for 10 minutes.

Serve hot or warm.

JOAN'S CARROT BREAD-CAKE

Preheat oven to 350 degrees

I make this recipe every time I do a holiday dinner!

1	stick sweet butter
1	stick margarine
¾	cup brown sugar
1	cup grated carrots
½	teaspoon salt
½	teaspoon baking soda
2	eggs
1½	cups flour
1	teaspoon baking powder
1	tablespoon water
1	tablespoon lemon juice

Melt butter and margarine in a small saucepan. Mix all the rest of the ingredients together in a large bowl. Add melted butter and margarine. Put mixture into a small tube shaped Jello mold that is sprayed with non-stick cooking spray. Bake in a preheated 350 degree oven for 45 minutes.

This recipe serves approximately 10 people. Cut small pieces because this is a very rich side dish!

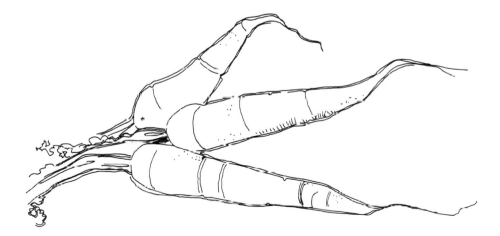

★ ★ ★ ★ ★ ★ ★ ★ ★ ★ ★ ★ ★ ★

BECKY BISOULIS' GREEK CHICKEN

★ ★ ★ ★ ★ ★ ★ ★ ★ ★ ★ ★ ★ ★ ★ ★ ★

Serves 8   *Preheat oven to 375 degrees*

Winner of the Chicago Gold Coast Award for the best new designer, Becky Bisoulis' designs are easy to wear and beautiful to look at. Whether in satins, lace and pearls or simple cottons, Ms. Bisoulis' designs are all winners and so is this delicious chicken!

3	**medium whole chickens**
8	**Idaho potatoes***
½	**cup olive oil**
1½	**sticks butter**
3	**lemons, cut into wedges**
	salt and pepper to taste
	lots and lots of oregano
⅓	**cup Reese's Tomato Marinade**

---

* If guests are Irish or Greek, allow one large potato per person, otherwise one small one will do.

1. Place scrubbed potatoes with skins on in the oven at 375 degrees and bake for 45 minutes.

2. While potatoes are baking, clean chickens and place in a large baking pan. (Pan should be large enough for the potatoes, also.)

3. Sprinkle chickens with olive oil and place chunks of butter inside and outside of chickens.

4. Squeeze the lemon wedges all over and leave some wedges inside the chickens and in the pan.

5. Sprinkle with salt and pepper to taste. Add liberal amounts of oregano inside and all over the chickens.

6. Reduce oven temperature to 325 degrees.

7. When potatoes are baked, remove from oven and slice about 1½ inches thick. Place them around chickens. There should be a nice amount of juice from chickens so you will be immersing potatoes into liquid.

8. About ½ hour before chickens are done (you will know doneness when chicken leg lifts easily from the joint and the skin is crispy brown) sprinkle ⅓ cup Reese's Tomato Marinade all over.

P.S. Add pan juices to each serving. Becky serves huge chunks of Greek bread, slightly toasted, to dip into the juices.

Becky says if you can't find Reese's Tomato Marinade, omit it.

★ ★ ★ ★ ★ ★ ★ ★ ★ ★

ARNOLD SCAASI'S CARIBBEAN CHICKEN

★ ★ ★ ★ ★ ★ ★ ★ ★ ★ ★ ★ ★ ★ ★ ★ ★ ★ ★ ★

Serves 4

Arnold Scaasi's elegant, entrance-making gowns have made him a sought after designer. Barbara Bush chose him to create her inaugural gown.

Arnold says of this recipe, "In the country, we use fresh farm chickens and double or triple the recipe for guests. In the city, it's dinner for four in my small dining room with its very large Dubuffet painting. I like the contrast of a simple, but flavorful dish, with a formal, beautifully set table and great art."

1	**chicken, quartered**
	flour
	salt and pepper
2	**tablespoons margarine**
6	**medium potatoes, peeled and quartered**
6	**large carrots, sliced, about ½ inch thick**
1	**medium yellow onion, chopped**
2	**10 ounce cans chicken broth**
½	**cup white wine**
	Tabasco sauce

Dust chicken lightly with flour and season with salt and pepper. Brown chicken in skillet on both sides in margarine (for 15 minutes), drain off fat. In separate pot, with boiling water, cook potatoes and carrots for ½ hour. Saute onions in separate deep skillet and add chicken broth, wine, salt, pepper and tabasco to taste. Add chicken and bring to a boil. Reduce heat and simmer slowly. Drain potatoes and carrots and add to large skillet with chicken and balance of ingredients. Simmer for approximately 1 hour and 15 minutes on low flame.

GRANDMA FRAN'S CHEESE PANCAKES

Yield: 8 medium pancakes

This recipe is always a favorite! My mother-in-law always has cottage cheese in her refrigerator for a last-minute meal.

1	**pound large or small curd cottage cheese**
2	**eggs**
¾-1	**cup flour**
	vegetable oil (for frying)
	sour cream and/or sugar (for topping)

In a medium size bowl, mix cottage cheese with eggs. Add flour, a little at a time, until the consistency is like pancake batter.

Using a large frying pan, cover the bottom with vegetable oil. Heat oil over medium temperature. When oil is hot, scoop large spoonfuls of batter into the pan. Turn once when golden brown. Drain on paper towels.

Serve with sour cream and sugar if desired. This is great with my egg salad or tuna salad.

This recipe can be doubled!

GLAZED CHICKEN

This chicken recipe is easy and delicious. I serve it with my mushroom rice ring.

1   **whole chicken, cut up**
    Lawry's Seasoned Salt to taste
1   **bottle Milani's 1890 French Salad Dressing**
1   **12 ounce jar apricot preserves**

Spray a 9 x 13 pan with non-stick cooking spray.

Season chicken with Lawry's seasoned salt and place skin side down in prepared pan. Broil until browned, then turn over and continue to broil until chicken is crispy. Combine dressing with preserves and pour over chicken.

Turn oven to 350 degrees and bake for an additional 30-45 minutes.

MUSHROOM RICE RING

1 pound rice (I use Uncle Ben's)
1 pint mushrooms, washed and sliced
1 can water chestnuts, sliced
¼ cup chopped green pepper or sliced pea pods
1 packet of beef bouillon
1 scrambled egg

Cook rice according to directions on package. Add all vegetables and stir in bouillon. Mix well.

Scramble an egg and add to rice mixture. Stir well to combine.

Spray a 6 cup ring mold with non-stick cooking spray and pat down rice mixture. Put in oven to keep warm until needed or refrigerate and then heat before serving.

Note: You can use Le Sueur peas or baby carrots glazed with brown sugar and butter in center of mold.

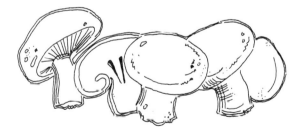

SPINACH NOODLE CASSEROLE

Serves 10   *Preheat oven to 350 degrees*

- ½   **pound fine egg noodles, cooked and drained**
- 1   **cup cottage cheese**
- 1   **cup sour cream**
-     **dash onion powder**
-     **dash garlic salt**
- 1   **tablespoon Worcestershire sauce**
- ½   **cup Parmesan cheese, grated**
- 2   **packages frozen Stouffer's Spinach Souffle, defrosted**

Mix together cottage cheese, sour cream, dash of onion powder and dash of garlic salt, Worcestershire sauce and Parmesan cheese. Add cooked and drained noodles and stir to coat.

Pour the noodle mixture into a greased 9 x 13 glass dish. Spread spinach souffle over top of noodles. Bake in a preheated 350 degree oven for 40 minutes. Cool slightly and spoon out individual servings or cut into squares. This recipe may be prepared in advance and frozen.

★ ★ ★ ★ ★ ★

BARRY AND CECE KIESELSTEIN-CORD'S
SWEET POTATO BASKETS

★ ★ ★ ★ ★ ★ ★ ★ ★ ★ ★ ★ ★ ★ ★ ★ ★ ★ ★ ★

Serves 6

Barry Kieselstein-Cord is a Coty award winning jewelry designer. His belts, earrings and accessories are all considered pieces of art. His wife, CeCe handles the art of cooking with the same degree of success! They are a wonderful pair in and out of the kitchen. This recipe originally appeared in the *New York Times Magazine.* It's a delicious side dish!

3	oranges
6	sweet potatoes
3	tablespoons butter
2	tablespoons brown sugar
½	cup pecans, chopped
3	ounces bourbon
1	package mini-marshmallows

1. Cut oranges in half and remove sections with grapefruit knife and spoon. (Save sections for breakfast or dessert.)

2. Scallop edges of oranges with paring knife and set aside.

3. Pare potatoes, place in saucepan, cover with water and cook until tender.

4. Drain potatoes, put through ricer or mash with potato masher. Beat in butter, sugar, pecans and bourbon. Mix well.

5. Fill orange shells with mashed potato mixture. Top with marshmallows.

6. Just before serving, place in oven to reheat, then place under broiler until marshmallows are just browned.

NEVER FROWN BRISKET

When most people hear brisket is being served, they usually make a sad face remembering their mother's brisket being greasy, fatty, stringy, or tough to chew. This recipe is a favorite for all generations!

6 **pounds brisket, first cut**
   Lawry's Seasoned Salt
1 **clove fresh garlic, minced**
1 **small jar Heinz chili sauce**
4 **tablespoons brown sugar**

I make sure that there is almost no fat on my brisket, so I have to trim it myself after the butcher gets finished trimming.

1. Place meat in shallow pan and sprinkle meat with seasoned salt on both sides.

2. Sprinkle minced garlic over one side of brisket and broil until top is brown, about 5 minutes. Turn over and repeat.

3. Turn over to original side and pour chili sauce over whole brisket. Fill empty chili jar ³/₄'s full of water and pour into shallow pan around the brisket.

4. Sprinkle brown sugar on top of chili sauce that is on top of brisket.

5. Cover tightly with foil paper and turn oven to 325 degrees and cook for 1¹/₂ hours.

6. Turn oven up to 350 degrees and continue cooking for an additional 1¹/₂ hours or until a fork comes out of meat easily.

7. Remove the excess liquid, scrape off brown sugar coating and put into a bowl in refrigerator to use later as gravy.

8. Slice brisket with an electric knife or take it to the butcher for a more professional job.

9. Pour gravy over brisket and heat in oven until warm, approximately 20-25 minutes.

SANDRA ROTH'S CARROT SOUFFLE

★ ★ ★ ★ ★ ★ ★ ★ ★ ★ ★ ★ ★ ★ ★ ★ ★ ★ ★ ★

Serves 8   *Preheat oven to 350 degrees*

Sandra is a well-known sportswear designer. Her CIAOSPORT label is a fashion favorite. Her souffle is sure to become a favorite, too.

¾	cup butter
¾	cup light shortening
1	cup dark brown sugar
2	cups flour
1	teaspoon baking soda
1	teaspoon salt
2	teaspoons baking powder
4	egg yolks
2	teaspoons lemon juice
2	tablespoons water
3	cups carrots, grated
5	egg whites

---

1. Cream butter and add shortening and sugar.

2. In separate bowl, mix flour, baking soda, salt and baking powder. Set aside.

3. Beat egg yolks until light in color. Add lemon juice, water and carrots.

4. Add flour mixture to butter mixture. Blend well. Add carrots.

5. In a separate bowl, beat egg whites until stiff. Fold egg whites into carrot mixture.

6. Pour into a greased 8 inch round casserole or souffle dish and bake for 1 hour and 10 minutes in a preheated 350 degree oven.

7. Test with a knife in the center. The knife must come out clean and dry.

AUNT LYLA'S KUGEL

Serves 24   *Preheat oven to 350 degrees*

I have eaten many noodle kugels in my time, but this is my favorite.

- **1   pound broad egg noodles, cooked and drained**
- **4   eggs, lightly beaten**
- **½   cup sugar**
- **1   pound cottage cheese**
- **1   20 oz. can crushed pineapple (#2 can), drained well**
- **1   8 ounce jar apricot preserves**
- **1   cup corn flakes crushed (or less)**
- **½   pound butter, melted**
- **1   tablespoon sugar (for garnish)**

Mix cooked noodles with eggs, sugar, cottage cheese, pineapple and preserves. Put mixture in a 9 x 13 pan sprayed with non-stick cooking spray. Cover mixture with crushed corn flakes and drizzle with melted butter. Sprinkle a little sugar over butter and bake in a preheated 350 degree oven for 1½ hours or until top is brown.

Cool slightly and cut into squares and serve.

This recipe freezes beautifully!

HOT OR COLD SALMON LOAF

Preheat oven to 350 degrees

I serve this when I make a dairy lunch at the show room.

1	**can salmon or tuna, drained**
2	**cups plain bread crumbs**
½	**cup milk**
1	**egg, well beaten**
1	**teaspoon salt**
1	**tablespoon parsley, finely chopped**
	dash of pepper
2	**tablespoons butter, melted**
1	**tablespoon lemon juice**

Flake fish and remove any bones. Add all ingredients together and mix well. Pour into an 8½ or 9 inch loaf pan sprayed with non-stick cooking spray. Set pan into another pan partially filled with water and bake in a preheated 350 degree oven for 40 minutes or until firm. Unmold and slice, or if serving cold, refrigerate for a few hours before serving.

This recipe can be prepared in advance and then frozen. Use the Easy Cucumber Sauce on the side.

MAGGIE'S MIXED UP VEGGIE CASSEROLE

Preheat oven to 350 degrees

2	packages frozen chopped broccoli, thaw and drain well
2	large cans cream style corn
2	tablespoons chopped onion
2	eggs (or egg whites) slightly beaten
½	stick margarine, melted
2	cups Pepperidge Farm Corn Bread stuffing
½	stick margarine, melted

Mix together broccoli, corn, onion, eggs and margarine and pour into a 9 x 13 casserole that has been sprayed with non-stick cooking spray. Spread vegetables out evenly to cover pan.

Sprinkle corn bread stuffing over vegetable mixture and drizzle with melted margarine.

Bake in a preheated 350 degree oven for 1 hour.

To serve, spoon out individual servings!

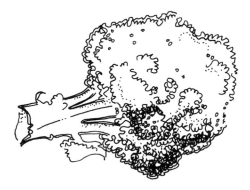

NOTES

NOTES

TIME FOR BREAKFAST

Time For Breakfast

GOOD MORNING (OR ANYTIME) COFFEE!

For the best coffee you'll ever taste, sprinkle 1 teaspoon of cinnamon on top of ground coffee for 12 cups of coffee. Add 2 drops of vanilla extract and stir just to blend.

For chocolaty flavor also add 1 teaspoon of unsweetened cocoa.

Brew and enjoy a cup of coffee sure to bring on the compliments.

GERMAN APPLE PANCAKE

Serves 2 people   *Preheat oven to 350 degrees*

¼ **cup sugar**
¼ **cup brown sugar**
1 **tablespoon of cinnamon**
4 **apples, sliced**
1 **stick butter or margarine**
½ **cup of flour**
½ **cup of milk**
½ **teaspoon of salt**

Spray an 8 or 9 inch round cake pan with non-stick cooking spray.

Combine sugar, brown sugar and cinnamon and sprinkle bottom of pan. Lay apple slices on top of sugar and cinnamon so there are enough apple slices to cover the bottom of the pan. Cut butter into small pieces and dot the apples.

Bake in a preheated 350 degree oven for 10 minutes.

Meanwhile, beat the flour, milk and salt together. Pour mixture on baked apples. Return to oven for an additional 15 minutes. Remove from oven and invert on a plate. Serve immediately. Delish!

OOPS!!! on page 208
ADD 2 eggs
BEAT eggs with flour, milk & salt

EGG SOUFFLE

Serves 4   *Preheat oven to 350 degrees*

  1   **small cream cheese**
½   **cup milk**
  8   **eggs**
  1   **tablespoon butter**
      salt & pepper to taste

Whip all ingredients together and pour into a 4 cup souffle dish sprayed with non-stick cooking spray. Bake 20 minutes in a preheated 350 degree oven.

Serve immediately.

JUDY'S BRUNCH COFFEE CAKE

When I was staying in L.A. a few years ago, my very dear friend Judy Tallarico made brunch for us one morning and served this cake. We couldn't stop eating it.

1   **bag whole pecans**
2   **frozen Rhodes breads (2 loaves in package), defrosted**
1   **package butterscotch pudding and pie filling, <u>not</u> instant**
½   **cup brown sugar**
1   **teaspoon cinnamon**
¼   **pound butter, melted**

---

1. Spray or grease a bundt pan and cover the bottom with the whole pecans.

2. Cut defrosted Rhodes Frozen breads into large pieces. Drop bread chunks on nuts.

3. Sprinkle the box of pudding on top of bread.

4. Sprinkle brown sugar on top of pudding layer.

5. Sprinkle a teaspoon of cinnamon on top of the brown sugar.

6. Drizzle melted butter over the brown sugar.

Put in the refrigerator overnight. In the morning, take out of refrigerator 3 hours before baking to let the dough rise. Bake for ½ hour in a preheated 350 degree oven. Remove from oven and wait 10 minutes, then invert on a plate. This cake must be eaten immediately.

BLUEBERRY FRUIT CRUNCH

This is a quick, easy and delicious coffee cake.

  1   **package Duncan Hines Blueberry Muffin mix**
 ¼ **cup butter**
  1   **can (1 pound 5 ounces) fruit pie filling**
      (choice of cherry, peach, apple, blueberry or pineapple)
 ½ **teaspoon cinnamon**
 ½ **teaspoon almond extract**
 ¼ **cup chopped nuts — walnuts or pecans**

In a small saucepan, melt butter and set aside to cool. Empty packaged blueberries into strainer and rinse under cold water. Set aside.

Pour fruit pie filling into an 8 or 9 inch square pan sprayed with non-stick cooking spray.

Combine cinnamon, almond extract and blueberries and sprinkle over pie filling. Add dry muffin mix and nuts to cool melted butter and combine with fork until crumbly. Distribute evenly over fruit in pan.

Bake in a preheated 350 degree oven for 30 - 40 minutes, until golden brown.

This cake is great served with ice cream or Cool Whip.

BANANA BREAD

Preheat oven to 350 degrees

When I first got married, 20 years ago, I made this recipe almost all the time. It's still a favorite today as a breakfast bread — or anytime!

1/3	**cup butter or margarine**
1/2	**cup sugar**
2	**eggs**
1 3/4	**cups sifted all purpose flour**
1	**teaspoon baking powder**
1/2	**teaspoon baking soda**
1 1/2	**cups ripe bananas, mashed**
1/2	**cup chopped walnuts or pecans (optional)**

Cream together butter and sugar; add eggs and beat well. Sift all dry ingredients together and add to creamed mixture on low speed. Blend in bananas and mix well. If desired, stir in nuts.

Pour into a well sprayed loaf pan (9 1/2 x 5 x 3). Bake for 40-45 minutes in a preheated 350 degree oven or until a toothpick comes out clean.

Cool for 1 hour before removing from pan.

Freezes well.

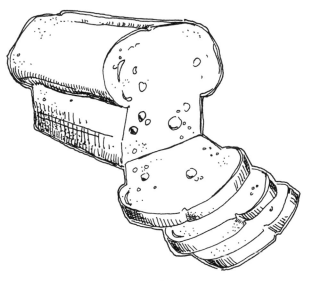

GREAT BLUEBERRY BREAKFAST CAKE

Preheat oven to 350 degrees

Cake:
- ¼ cup butter
- ¾ cup sugar
- 1 egg
- ½ cup milk
- 2 cups flour
- 2 teaspoons baking powder
- 2 cups fresh blueberries (toss with some flour so berries won't sink)

Topping:
- ¼ cup butter
- ½ cup sugar
- ⅓ cup flour
- ½ teaspoon cinnamon

In a mixer, cream butter and sugar. Add egg and milk and mix well. Slowly add flour and baking powder. By hand, fold in floured blueberries. Pour batter into a greased 8 or 9 inch square pan.

Prepare topping by placing all the ingredients in a bowl and cutting with a pastry knife or fork to make a crumbly mixture. Sprinkle on top of batter and bake in a preheated 350 degree oven for 35 minutes.

Freezes well.

BREAKFAST BARS

I like these early in the morning, but they are wonderful any time of the day.

1	**8 ounce package of chopped pitted dates**
1	**cup raisins**
1	**cup walnuts or pecans, chopped**
1	**teaspoon grated orange peel (optional)**
2	**teaspoons cinnamon**
1	**cup sugar**
1/4	**pound butter (or margarine)**
1	**teaspoon vanilla extract**
2	**eggs**
2	**cups all purpose flour**
2	**teaspoons baking powder**
2	**tablespoons orange juice**
	confectioners sugar to garnish

Grease 2 cookie sheets and set aside.

In a large bowl, mix together dates, raisins, walnuts and orange peel. Mix 1/2 cup sugar with the cinnamon. Pour over fruits and nuts and stir, making sure they are well coated. In a separate bowl, cream butter and remaining 1/2 cup of sugar and vanilla extract until light and fluffy. Beat in eggs, one at a time. Stir in flour, baking powder and orange juice. Add fruit and nut mixture and beat until well blended. The dough will be stiff.

Shape into logs, 2 on each cookie sheet. Bake 15-20 minutes in a preheated 350 degree oven until bars are light brown. They will seem soft, but will firm up as they cool. When cool, cut diagonally into 3/4 inch bars. Sprinkle with confectioners sugar.

DIET BRAN MUFFINS

Yield: 4 muffins   *Preheat oven to 350 degrees*

8	tablespoons Millers Bran
3	tablespoons powdered skim milk
½	teaspoon cinnamon
1	packet of Sweet 'N Low or Equal
3	tablespoons water
1	egg
½	teaspoon vanilla extract
1	apple, sliced and then cut into small chunks

In a small bowl combine by hand the bran, powdered milk, cinnamon and sugar substitute. Stir in water, egg and vanilla extract to moisten. DO NOT OVERBEAT. Add apples and stir just to cover.

Spray 4 muffin cups with non-stick cooking spray or line with paper cups. Fill them ½ full with batter and bake for 25 minutes in a preheated 350 degree oven.

These muffins are only good for one day. That's why I only make 4. But if you need more double the recipe.

RASPBERRY MELTAWAY MUFFINS

Yield: 24 mini muffins   *Preheat oven to 350 degrees*

These muffins will melt in your mouth!

¾	**cups (1½ sticks) well chilled unsalted butter**
¼	**cup sugar**
1	**tablespoon sour cream**
1	**teaspoon vanilla extract**
¼	**teaspoon salt (optional)**
1½	**cups flour**
¼	**to ½ cup raspberry preserves**
	confectioners sugar

Cream butter and sugar. Add sour cream, vanilla extract and salt. Mix until well blended. Add flour and blend well.

Take 1 tablespoon of dough and form small ball and press into mini muffin tins, sprayed with non-stick cooking spray. Bake in a preheated 350 degree oven for about 25 minutes.

Remove from oven and let cool for 5-10 minutes. Remove from muffin tins and cover the top of each with ½ teaspoon of raspberry preserves. Place each into mini-muffin papers. Dust with confectioners sugar.

This recipe freezes well.

NOTES

NOTES

BUFFET ACCESSORIES

Buffet Accessories

★ ⋆ ☆ ★ ★ ⋆ ⋆ ⋆ ★ ⋆ ⋆ ⋆ ⋆ ⋆ ★ ★ ★ ⋆ ⋆ ⋆

CAROLYNE ROEHM'S OMELETTE SOUFFLE
AU GRAND MARNIER

★ ★ ★ ★ ★ ★ ★ ★ ★ ★ ★ ★ ★ ★ ★ ★ ★ ★ ★ ★

Serves 6   *Preheat oven to 400 degrees*

Carolyne Roehm got her start as an assistant to Oscar De La Renta. Now she stands firmly on her own two feet... but she's never caught standing around. Sophisticated and elegant women seek out her couture gowns and fabulous sportswear. This dessert is a light and refreshing way to end a special dinner.

6   individual omelette pans (copper is recommended)

6   egg yolks
7   egg whites
2   tablespoons super fine sugar
¼   cup English marmalade
10   tablespoons Grand Marnier
     confectioners sugar
6   candied violets, optional
6   mint sprigs, optional

Beat egg yolks with whisk until frothy. Add super fine sugar to taste. Blend in marmalade. Add 2-4 tablespoons Grand Marnier to taste. Whisk all ingredients, just to blend.

Dust omelette pans with super fine sugar. Place 1 tablespoon Grand Marnier in bottom of each. In a separate bowl, whip egg whites until stiff peaks begin to form. Gently, fold in yolk mixture, just until incorporated. Be careful not to break the egg whites. Mixture will be lumpy.

Carefully spoon into pans. Gently stir before each serving to keep ingredients properly combined. Bake in a preheated 400 degree oven for 6 minutes, or until golden on top. The edges will be lightly done and the inside will be moist.

To serve, dust with confectioners sugar and garnish with violet and mint sprig.

*Since the copper pans are very hot, Carolyne suggests putting a pretty napkin on the serving plate to prevent it from cracking.

GLAZED PARTY NUTS

Preheat oven to 325 degrees

These are my "famous" party nuts that I make for every market and for all my dinner parties. This simple recipe is sure to impress your guests!

   2   egg whites
   1   cup sugar
       pinch of salt
   2   pounds walnuts or pecans

Beat egg whites into peaks while slowly adding sugar and salt. Carefully fold in nuts.

Spray cookie sheet with non-stick cooking spray. Spread sugar-glazed nuts in a single layer on the pan.

Bake in a preheated 325 degree oven for 20 minutes. Turn nuts and bake for an additional 20 minutes or until dry.

Cool completely and place in an airtight container. They will keep fresh for weeks!

P.S. If you want a cinnamon-flavored nut, just add a teaspoon of cinnamon to the egg and sugar mixture.

ANN LAWRENCE'S DAVINITY

★ ★ ★ ★ ★ ★ ★ ★ ★ ★ ★ ★ ★ ★ ★ ★ ★ ★ ★ ★

Ann Lawrence is truly a "divine" designer. She creates wonderful dresses and gowns for those special, enchanted evenings. This recipe for a white candy, similar to fudge was handed down to her by her family who were bakers and candy makers in Arizona.

2	cups sugar
1/2	cup water
1/2	cup white corn syrup
2	egg whites
3/4	cup cherries, drained (optional)
3	tablespoons lemon extract
3/4	cup almonds, blanched

In a saucepan, heat sugar, water and corn syrup, watching carefully while stirring. Bring to a boil (do not scorch). Beat egg whites until dry. Then pour sugar mixture into egg whites while continuing to beat. Beat until fairly dry, white and fluffy. Add cherries (optional), lemon extract and almonds. Stir.

Pour onto a greased pan or wax paper lined platter.

Cut into squares when candy has set. Eat and enjoy.

★ ★

ELEANOR P. BRENNER'S COLD LEMON SOUFFLE

★ ★ ★ ★ ★ ★ ★ ★ ★ ★ ★ ★ ★ ★ ★ ★ ★ ★ ★ ★

Eleanor P. Brenner has become one of the Shining Stars of 7th Avenue and one of our closest friends. Eleanor is known as one of America's leading fashion designers. She is also the author of the *Gourmet Cooking Without Salt* cookbook. This Lemon Souffle is one of her favorites and I know it will be one of yours!

1¼	cups cold water
2	packages unflavored gelatin
3⅓	cups heavy cream
1	teaspoon vanilla extract (optional)
8	large eggs, separated, at room temperature
1¾	cups sugar
¾	cup lemon juice = juice of 4 large, fresh lemons
2	tablespoons lemon rind, finely grated
¼	teaspoon cream of tartar

Garnish:
⅔	cup heavy cream, whipped with
1½	tablespoons confectioners sugar

───────────────────────

1. Prepare a 2 quart souffle dish with a 5 inch souffle collar. Spray the inside with non-stick cooking spray.

2. Place water in the top of a double boiler and sprinkle the gelatin on top of water to soften.

3. Using electric mixer on medium high speed, whip the cream with the vanilla extract until stiff peaks hold their shape. Refrigerate.

4. Fill bottom of double boiler with water to within one inch from top part. Turn flame to medium and bring water to scalding point. Turn the flame low. Place the top part of the double boiler into the bottom and cook for 3 to 4 minutes. (Water in bottom part should not boil.) Turn the flame off.

5. Using an electric mixer on medium speed, beat the egg yolks with the sugar until they are thick, creamy and a pale, yellow color. Slowly add the gelatin mixture, beating all the time, until the gelatin is totally absorbed into the egg yolk-sugar-lemon mixture.

6. In a separate bowl using the electric mixer on high speed, beat the egg whites and cream of tartar until stiff but not dry.

7. Using a rubber spatula, mix ¼ of the egg whites into the egg yolk mixture, then fold in the remainder of the egg whites.

8. Fold the whipped cream into the egg mixture.

9. Spoon the mixture into the souffle dish and refrigerate at least 24 hours.

To serve: Cover the souffle top with whipped cream, remove collar, serve immediately on a doily covered silver tray.

NIBBLE AND MUNCH

My friend Denise from L.A. gave me this recipe. It's great for a large group of people who like to snack.

- 1 stick butter
- ⅓ cup + ¼ teaspoon Worcestershire sauce
- ¼ teaspoon garlic powder
- ¼ teaspoon Mrs. Dash seasoning
  dash mild chili powder

- 2 cups of each:
  Wheat Chex
  Rice Chex
  Cheerios
  thin pretzel sticks
  dry roasted mixed nuts

Melt butter and combine with Worchestershire sauce, garlic powder, Mrs. Dash's seasoning and chili powder.

In a large bowl, combine all the cereals and nuts. Toss with ½ of the seasoning mixture and ½ of cereal. Pour into a 9 x 13 pan. Repeat with other ½ of cereal and seasoning. Toss.

Bake in a 350 degree oven for 45 minutes. Mix while baking.

Cool and store in container. Can also be frozen.

JAMES GALANOS' FAVORITE RECIPE!

James Galanos is the California Star of American Couture. When my dear friend, Judy Tallarico, asked her good friend Jimmy for his favorite recipe to be included in my cookbook, he replied with a laugh . . . "I don't cook! I enjoy eating in the newest and most exciting restaurants of the moment." You'll find this recipe easy to follow and a treat to prepare!

★ ★ ★ ☆ ☆ ★ ☆ ☆ ★ ★ ☆ ☆ ★ ☆ ☆ ☆ ☆ ☆

CAROLINA HERRERA'S CHOCOLATE MOUSSE

★ ★ ★ ★ ★ ★ ★ ★ ★ ★ ★ ★ ★ ★ ★ ★ ★ ★

Serves 12

Carolina Herrera has made an outstanding contribution to the field of fashion design. Her creations are chic and elegant. The women who wear her clothes love the way they look and feel. This mousse recipe is delicious! Carolina says, "I adore chocolate and enjoy collecting recipes!" Her husband, Reinaldo adds, "My wife is very good at 'giving directions' in the kitchen, but I would not trust her to boil an egg with her own hands."

½	**pound bittersweet chocolate**
½	**pound butter**
3	**eggs**

Grate chocolate and melt with butter in double boiler. Remove from heat the moment it is melted. Do not allow it to cook. Let cool.

Separate eggs. Beat egg yolks until frothy. Slowly add cooled chocolate and stir well with a wooden spoon.

Beat egg white until firm. Add chocolate mixture, a little at a time, stirring continuously. Pour mixture into 12, 4 ounce pot-de-cremes. Chill in refrigerator.

This dessert is best prepared the day before serving.

FUN WITH CANDY MELTING CHOCOLATE

Buy any color candy melting chocolate. I buy white chocolate bark that is used for candy making or chocolate discs which I melt in a double boiler or a microwave oven. When melted I dip:

Oreo cookies
pretzels, any kind
marshmallows, with thin pretzel sticks or sucker sticks as stems
chocolate wafer cookies

For M&Ms and M&M peanuts, pour candy into chocolate, stir and pour onto wax paper to cool. Then break apart. For an added treat, add crushed Oreo cookies to the mixture.

P. S. For a really cute party idea, purchase tiny ice cream cones, with the pointed bottoms, from a candy store. Take a whole marshmallow, cut it in half and place in opening of cone (like a scoop of ice cream). Dip the cone into melted chocolate so just the marshmallow top is covered. Then sprinkle the wet chocolate with multi-colored non-pareils.

To display, I take a slab of Styrofoam and take the eraser side of a pencil and stab rows of holes. Then I insert cones so they stand up.

FANCY PLATE DECORATION

Bonnie Rabert, our fabulous food stylist, used this trick to decorate the plate of Caesar Salad Pasta on the cover of the book. She taught me the technique, and I thought I'd pass it on.

Using a plate with at least a 1½ inch wide rim, hold a stick of butter like a felt-tip pen and use it to coat rim. Use about ½ teaspoon of butter. Place a piece of wax paper under plate. Sprinkle rim with 1½ tablespoons of appropriate garnish. Turn plate while sprinkling to get even coverage.

Clean exterior edge of plate with paper towel to give a finished, even look.

Garnish options:
> **parsley**
> **Parmesan cheese**
> **breadcrumbs**
> **paprika**
> **cocoa**

ELLIE'S PARTY PITA BREAD

These little "pick-ups" are great as appetizers or served with a main course.

1	**package Pita bread**
¼	**pound butter, softened**
	Parmesan cheese, grated
	Garlic powder
	oregano
	sesame seeds

Cut Pita bread into two round pieces. Break each half into quarters. Lightly spread rough side of bread with butter. Sprinkle with Parmesan cheese and garlic powder. If desired, sprinkle with oregano and/or sesame seeds.

Place under broiler, until just brown and bubbly. Watch carefully to prevent burning. Serve warm. These toasts can be kept for 3 days if put into an air-tight container.

★ ⠄⠄ ★ ★ ⠄ ★ ★ ⠄ ⠄ ⠄ ★ ★ ⠄ ⠄ ⠄ ★ ★

MARK HEISTER'S COLD CUCUMBER SOUP

★ ★ ★ ★ ★ ★ ★ ★ ★ ★ ★ ★ ★ ★ ★ ★ ★ ★

Chicago's own dapper designer Mark Heister not only creates timeless ensembles but leads his day to day life as a Renaissance man. He's made his mark in the fashion world not only as a Gold Coast Fashion awardee but was also honored by the Chicago Historical Society in a one man retrospective of his fashions.

Serves 4

2	**tablespoons butter**
¼	**cup onion, chopped**
	OR
1	**leek, unpeeled and diced.**
1	**cup watercress leaves, chopped**
½	**cup potato, finely diced**
2	**cups chicken broth**
2	**sprigs parsley**
¼	**teaspoon salt**
¼	**teaspoon freshly ground black pepper**
¼	**teaspoon dry mustard**
1	**cup heavy cream**
	for garnish: chives, chopped
	cucumbers, chopped
	radishes, chopped

In sauce pan melt butter. Add onion and cook until transparent. Add all remaining ingredients except cream and garnish vegetables and bring to boil. Simmer fifteen minutes or until potatoes are tender.

Purée in electric blender or put mixture through food mill and, if desired, through sieve or cheesecloth. Add more seasonings to taste. Chill in refrigerator.

Before serving, stir in cream. Garnish with chives, cucumber and radishes. Soup will be thick. It is suggested that it be served in parfait glasses with radish roses and garnishes.

ELLEN'S "STAFF OF LIFE"

Here's a recipe that's quick, cheap, delicious, healthy and portable. Ellen says, "You can eat as much as you like and still fit into your Scaasi's, Mackie's, Galanos' - or favorite pair of blue jeans!"

- **1 cup popcorn, preferably blue corn or "Black Diamond"**
- **3 tablespoons vegetable oil**
- **popcorn salt**

In a 3 quart saucepan, heat oil to 400 degrees. Add popcorn, cover and shake vigorously for 3 minutes, or until popping ceases. Immediately remove from heat and pour into large bowl. Cool, then sprinkle with popcorn salt. DON'T EVEN THINK ABOUT BUTTERING IT. Serve with a Diet Coke.

VANILLA SAUCE

Yield ½ cups

This sauce is a delicious topping for fancy souffles and simple brownies.

- **½ cup butter or margarine**
- **1 cup sugar**
- **½ cup light cream**
- **1 teaspoon vanilla extract**

Melt butter in medium saucepan. Remove from heat. Add sugar, cream and vanilla. Mix well. Simmer over low heat for 5 minutes. Keep stirring until sugar is dissolved and sauce is heated through. Serve immediately.

CHOCOLATE SOUFFLE

Serves 6-8   *Preheat oven to 425 degrees*

When we were first married, Barry used to make this dessert whenever we entertained.

4	tablespoons butter
1/4	cup sugar, for coating casserole
1	cup milk
2	1 ounce squares unsweetened chocolate
1/3	cup flour
1/4	teaspoon salt
4	eggs, separated
1/3	cup sugar
1	teaspoon vanilla extract
1/4	teaspoon almond extract
	whipped cream, for garnish
	Vanilla Sauce, for garnish (see recipe)

Liberally grease 1 1/2 quart casserole with butter. Sprinkle bottom and sides with sugar until just coated.

In double boiler, heat 1/2 cup milk with chocolate. Stir until melted. Beat until smooth with egg beater. In a separate bowl, mix flour, salt and remainder of milk. Stir into chocolate. Continue stirring and cook over medium heat until mixture is very thick. Remove from heat and beat until smooth.

Add egg yolks, one at a time, beating after each addition. Cover and set aside. With electric mixer, beat egg whites until small peaks form. Slowly add 1/3 cup sugar and continue to beat until stiff. Fold in chocolate mixture and extracts. Pour into prepared casserole.

Bake in a preheated 425 degree oven for 20 30 minutes. To test for doneness, poke a knife 1/2 way down in center of souffle. Knife should come out dry.

Serve immediately with whipped cream or Vanilla Sauce on the side.

COLD STRAWBERRY SOUP

Serves 4

3	cups strawberries, washed - cut off stems
1½	cups water
1½	cups white wine
½	cup sugar
2	tablespoons fresh lemon juice
1½	teaspoons corn starch
1½	tablespoons cold water
3	teaspoons lemon rind, grated
½	cup sour cream
	fresh strawberries, for garnish

Thinly slice strawberries. Place in 3 quart saucepan. Combine with water and wine. Cover and simmer for 10 minutes. Add sugar and lemon juice. Stir to blend. Combine corn starch with cold water. Pour into mixture and blend well. Over medium heat, bring to a boil. Stir just until thickened.

Pour into blender. Add lemon rind and sour cream. Whip until light pink in color. Cool completely. Add additional sugar to taste. Chill in refrigerator four hours or overnight. Stir to blend before serving. Pour into individual bowls and top with fresh sliced strawberries. A delicious summer treat!

MARLEY'S SWEET BAR-B-QUE SAUCE

This delicious sauce was given to me by my proofreader, Marley. It's an old family recipe that was handed down to her. She was so "sweet" to share it with me! This recipe can easily be doubled or tripled. It keeps in the refrigerator up to one month.

1	12 ounce bottle chili sauce
½	bottle water
½	cup brown sugar
1	medium onion, diced
⅛	cup vinegar
⅛	cup Worcestershire sauce
	salt
	pepper
	garlic powder
	paprika

Pour chili sauce in a medium saucepan. Using emptied bottle, fill half full with water. Shake to pick up leftover sauce and pour into saucepan. Add brown sugar, onion, vinegar, and Worcestershire sauce. Sprinkle salt, pepper, garlic powder and paprika to taste. Mix well, and simmer 30-40 minutes. Stir occasionally.

Cool and store in refrigerator. Great on chicken and ribs! Be sure to brush on sauce at end of grilling time. Watch closely to prevent burning.

HERBED FRESH TOMATO SOUP

Serves 8

This soup makes a beautiful presentation at an elegant dinner party. It's also a favorite when served plain at a family dinner.

2	tablespoons butter or margarine
2	tablespoons olive oil
2	medium onions, thinly sliced
1	6 ounce can tomato paste
2	tablespoons fresh basil, chopped
4	tablespoons fresh thyme, chopped
2	pounds fresh tomatoes, peeled, seeded, quartered (approximately 5 cups)
3	cups chicken broth
1	teaspoon salt
⅛	teaspoon pepper
2	packets artificial sweetener
	whipped cream
	fresh thyme or basil, chopped

In large saucepan, combine butter or margarine and olive oil. Over medium heat, cook until butter melts. Add onions and cook until tender, but not brown. Stir in tomato paste, basil and thyme. Mash fresh tomatoes and add to mixture. Pour in chicken broth. Mix well.

Bring to a boil. Reduce heat and cover. Simmer for 40 minutes. Press through food mill, sieve or puree in blender.

Return soup to saucepan. Stir in salt, pepper and sweetener. Heat to serve. Pour into individual bowls and garnish with dollop of whipped cream. Sprinkle with pinch of chopped herbs.

This makes a delicious light meal when accompanied by a tossed salad and garlic bread.

MAUREEN'S SPAGHETTI SAUCE

This delicious, full-bodied sauce is a family recipe passed down to my friend Maureen. It's terrific on pasta, grilled veal chops or baked eggplant!

3	pounds ground meat
2	tablespoons garlic, minced
1	pound medium onions
3-4	green peppers, chopped
1	pound fresh mushrooms, sliced
2	8 ounce cans whole tomatoes
2	8 ounce cans tomato sauce
2	8 ounce cans stewed tomatoes
3	packages dry spaghetti sauce mix
½	cup sugar
⅓	cup parsley, chopped
1½	teaspoons Accent
1½	teaspoons salt
1½	teaspoons Italian seasoning
1	teaspoon garlic powder
1	teaspoon allspice
1	teaspoon nutmeg
1	teaspoon pepper

In a large frying pan, brown meat with garlic, onions, green peppers and mushrooms. Drain all fat. Add canned tomatoes, tomato sauce, stewed tomatoes and dry spaghetti sauce mix. Stir to blend well. Add rest of ingredients. Simmer for 90 minutes, uncovered, stirring occasionally. Add more tomato paste to thicken.

This sauce freezes well.

JANET'S FROTHY FINALE

Serves 4-6

- 1 **pint lemon sherbet, softened**
- 1 **pint pineapple sherbet, softened**
- 1 **pint French vanilla ice cream, softened**
     DO NOT SUBSTITUTE ice milk or frozen yogurt
- 1½ **tablespoons grated lemon zest (2 lemons)**
- 1 **tablespoon Cointreau**
- 1 **tablespoon Grand Marnier**
- 2 **1 ounce squares semi-sweet chocolate, finely grated**
- 2 **1 ounce squares milk chocolate, finely grated**
  small fresh flowers, for garnish
  mint leaves, for garnish

Blend sherbets and ice cream until creamy. Add grated lemon zest and blend well.
Add Cointreau and Grand Marnier, adding more to taste. Stir until well blended.
Pour into small mixing bowl and cover. Put in freezer for several hours or
overnight.

Remove from freezer 30 minutes before serving. Beat into frothy texture. Spoon
into individual champagne flutes or parfait glasses. Form top into peak and top
with a sprinkling of both chocolates. Garnish with a fresh flower and a mint leaf.

ILENE AND STEVE'S HOT FUDGE

Serves 4-6

- ½ **cup granulated sugar**
- 2 **1 ounce squares semi-sweet chocolate**
- 4 **tablespoons milk**
- 2 **tablespoons dark corn syrup**
- ¼ **teaspoon vanilla extract**
- 2 **tablespoons butter**

Place all ingredients in small saucepan and cook on low-medium heat. Slowly stir
with rubber or wooden spoon and continue to cook until all chocolate has been
melted. Bring to a slow boil and continue to cook and stir until desired thickness.
(The longer it cooks the thicker it becomes.) Serve over your favorite ice cream.

★ ★ ★ ★ ★ ★ ★ ★ ★ ★ ★ ★

BOB MACKIE'S LATE NIGHT PIG OUT!

★ ★ ★ ★ ★ ★ ★ ★ ★ ★ ★ ★ ★ ★ ★ ★ ★

Bob Mackie is known as the "King of Glitter!" His gorgeous gowns are sought after by the biggest names in Hollywood. In fact, there isn't a woman who doesn't feel glamorous in one of his fabulous creations! Bob says, "This is the recipe that made me what I am today."

1. Take one half pint of Haagen Daaz "Vanilla Swiss Almond" ice cream.

2. Sit down in front of TV.

3. Open carton and eat with large spoon.

4. Finish the entire contents.

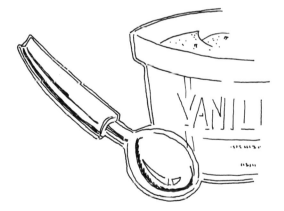

NOTES

INDEX

MY FAVORITE RECIPES

MY FAVORITE RECIPES

MY FAVORITE RECIPES

MY FAVORITE RECIPES

COOKIE STAGMAN'S

BEAUTIFUL BUFFETS!

c/o Platinum Publications
P.O. Box 3159
Chicago, Illinois 60654

Please send me _____ copies of BEAUTIFUL BUFFETS
           at $22.95 each $_____
       plus shipping/handling at $ 2.50 each $_____
add sales tax for delivery in Illinois
           at $ 1.84 each $_____
please furnish gift enclosure card
           at $ .50 each $_____
           TOTAL $_____

Name _____

Address _____

City _____ State _____ Zip _____

All copies will be sent to the same address unless otherwise specified. If you wish one or any number of books sent as gifts, furnish a list of names and addresses of recipients. If you wish to enclose your own gift card with each book, please write name of recipient on outside of envelope, enclose with order, and we will include it with your gift.

Make checks or money orders payable to Platinum Publications or charge to   ☐ VISA ☐ MASTERCARD

_ _ _ _ - _ _ _ _ - _ _ _ _ - _ _ _ _

EXPIRATION _____
PRINTED NAME ON CARD _____
SIGNATURE _____

Prices subject to change.

- -

COOKIE STAGMAN'S

BEAUTIFUL BUFFETS!

c/o Platinum Publications
P.O. Box 3159
Chicago, Illinois 60654

Please send me _____ copies of BEAUTIFUL BUFFETS
           at $22.95 each $_____
       plus shipping/handling at $ 2.50 each $_____
add sales tax for delivery in Illinois
           at $ 1.84 each $_____
please furnish gift enclosure card
           at $ .50 each $_____
           TOTAL $_____

Name _____

Address _____

City _____ State _____ Zip _____

All copies will be sent to the same address unless otherwise specified. If you wish one or any number of books sent as gifts, furnish a list of names and addresses of recipients. If you wish to enclose your own gift card with each book, please write name of recipient on outside of envelope, enclose with order, and we will include it with your gift.

Make checks or money orders payable to Platinum Publications or charge to   ☐ VISA ☐ MASTERCARD

_ _ _ _ - _ _ _ _ - _ _ _ _ - _ _ _ _

EXPIRATION _____
PRINTED NAME ON CARD _____
SIGNATURE _____

Prices subject to change.